To Malcolm & ~~Steve~~

With love from

Karen.

11th November 2004

Happy Christmas to
you both from us
both!
Karen & Jan.

Mothmilk and Moondust

This book comes to being as near a ray of sunshine as is humanly possible. The poems 'Hope' and 'Death of Olwen' gave me comfort, having recently been widowed. Amid many descriptions of suffering, I was, on finishing the book, full of optimism.

Dr Winnie Ewing,
President, Scottish National Party

Duncan McCuaig

MOTHMILK AND MOONDUST

Karen McCuaig Macdonald

Covenanters

Published by
Covenanters Press

the joint imprint of
Zeticula
57 St Vincent Crescent
Glasgow
G3 8NQ
and
Scottish Christian Press
21 Young Street
Edinburgh
EH2 4HU

http://www.covenanters.co.uk
admin@covenanters.co.uk

ISBN 1 905022 04 2 Paperback
ISBN 1 905022 05 0 Hardback

I would like to dedicate this collection
to my late mother,

Olwen Drysdale,

whose beauty and strength were not only on the
outside, but gave her a presence and a fortitude which
steadied us all on our journey through life, and whose
courage in the face of bereavements and cancer were
an inspiration and support to all who met her, not
least those who looked after her so faithfully when she
stayed in Strathcarron Hospice.

*With love
from
Karen*

Acknowledgements

Thanks are owed to *The Herald* for permission to reprint **Dancing with Ghosts,** which first appeared in *The Glasgow Herald* in 1996.

And to *The Milngavie and Bearsden Herald*, for permission to reprint the two poems **Again and Again** and **Answer to Again and Again,** *which first appeared there in 1998*

And last, but not least, thanks to Frances Ennis, who wrote **Again and Again,** for her permission to include her poem.

Duck pond at Strathcarron

Contents

Foreword

"Your sons and daughters will prophesy, your old men will dream dreams, your young men will see visions." Joel 2: 28.

The bath is a wonderful place. Perhaps it's because that's where I'm nearer to that state of closeness to where I came from that I'm more open to God's voice and inspiration. In the warm caress of steaming hot water I let go of the day's busyness, the clamour of the phone and the fragmented thoughts of what I ought to be doing instead of whatever it is that I'm doing now.

I started life in the middle of a wartime romance that was as poignant and bittersweet as any that you have watched on the silver screen, a time when all the young men were heroes, brave and handsome in uniform, and all the young women were beautiful heroines. Dangerous Moonlight and Dam Busters, Pearl Harbour and Saving Private Ryan. For me, the drone of Spitfires overhead, taking off and landing at the nearby airfield, along with the roar of waves breaking at the foot of Cornish cliffs, was the lullaby that sent me to sleep in my pram. That story is described in "Dancing With Ghosts: 'R' 'U' Confused". It's all part of what makes me 'me', and perhaps explains why I spent so much of my life searching for my identity.

Many years later, after a wonderful childhood, I was about to become a grandmother when my beloved mother Olwen was diagnosed with cancer. The diagnosis had been a long time in coming, and perhaps it was a relief, as we had known for a while that there was something seriously wrong with her. She had been suffering excruciating back pain, and no one could come up with a better answer than 'wear and tear' and 'just take more co-dydromol' … hardly the solution to the onslaught of bone cancer; and then there came the day when her legs started to give way beneath her and she was no longer able to live at home. Now, with the diagnosis of cancer, there could be effective treatment for the pain at least, and in fact, cobalt therapy at the Beatson Institute here in Glasgow brought considerable improvement and bought her several years more time with us. She had moved in to live with my sister in Dollar, the little town where I grew up, and was having wonderful home support from a MacMillan nurse based at Strathcarron Hospice in Denny, Stirlingshire. She had several periods of respite care in Strathcarron, and latterly went for daycare there once a week. She just loved the peace and moral support she found in Strathcarron. She loved the ducks in the pond outside her window too! I got the feeling that they loved her as much as she loved them …. the staff, I mean, not the ducks!!!

So there I was, lying in the bath, having a deep conversation with God about my mother's healing. Like so many before me and after me, I was asking big, big questions about healing, the whys and why-nots of this perennial learning curve.

Quite unexpectedly I had a very clear vision of someone I took to be my mother, sitting in her living-room at a table, and she was writing a book.

'But Lord,' I protested, 'that can't be right. Forgive me for saying so, but my mother *paints*, she doesn't write.'

I knew that she had at one point intended to start a new career in writing, but that was in 1945 when, as a newly widowed young mother she had to think of a way to support herself and little me. However, ever since I had been old enough to be aware of my mother's talents, she was following in her father's and mother's artistic footsteps and painting, that is, when she had time, as six children didn't leave a lot of that commodity. Sometimes she painted in oils, lots of watercolours, and some drawings and other media too. She will be remembered by many for the paintings of flowers that she did to raise funds as a way of thanking Strathcarron for their loving care.

Meanwhile, during my mother's six years of illness, my husband and I started a small wholesale sandwich production business. That was a steep learning curve too, and we found ourselves working a 90-hour week. 'They abolished slavery and brought in self-employment to replace it' had been quoted to us, and I did indeed feel that was the case at times, although I wouldn't have missed the experience for anything, and value the friendships we made then.

The business had a computer which was ostensibly for producing labels for the sandwiches. 'You won't have time to use it for anything else,' I was told. That's where they were wrong! I quickly discovered that the computer was my stress-buster and my sanity. During the quiet period in the afternoon, while I was supposed to be doing the dreaded cleaning down of every surface in sight, I found myself stealing time to write. What a joy it was, to pour out ideas and dreams onto this wonderful gadget, the 'word preciser' that allowed me to write precisely what I was thinking, feeling and seeing. I invented the expression 'word pictures' because I began to understand that what my mother was able to put on paper with brush and paint I could put into words.

When Ian's and my thirtieth wedding anniversary came around, I was able to give him 'The Island', a composite 'word-picture' of all the joyful holidays we had had on North Uist over many years. I did feel guilty as I wrote it in secret, as to do so I had to steal hours out of cleaning down time and that made more work for Ian at the end of each long day. However, since he was always much faster than me at the job (I'm such a perfectionist!), it worked well, and my guilt vanished when I saw the tears of happiness in his eyes on reading the finished story.

I showed my mother the story, and she loved it too. She also read some other stuff I wrote, and her comment was that she was sure I would get into print some day. I can't tell you how much that comment meant to me!

However, life went on and the sad day came when Olwen slipped the bonds of this earth and went to join her beloved Duncan and Douglas. It was hardly a surprise, but nonetheless it was a shock to the system. One never believes that the day will actually come.

Four months later my first poem came to me, needless to say, in the bath! I could hardly wait to get out of the bath and get to the word-processor to put the words down as they flowed thick and fast. That was when I began to wonder whether my vision had been of my mother, or was it in fact a vision of what God had planned for me?

The years have flown by since then, with poems and essays coming to me in fits and starts, usually two or three at a time then none for a while. I kept waiting 'to be discovered', until several friends leaned on me very hard and told me I 'had to' get into print.

I can only think that God himself has directed this production, as it has all happened 'to me' rather than 'by me'. Since He gave me the talent, I look to Him for the best way forward, and pray that the words I have written will bring hope and comfort to many people, with the occasional smile thrown in for good measure, and in some small way help to raise funds for Strathcarron Hospice. May my 'word pictures' do the same as my mother's paintings, and point people to our great Creator God and His Son, the Lord Jesus

Tranquillity at Strathcarron

Part 1

Endings and Beginnings

Death of Olwen

The sands of time were running out
For the one we loved,
And we could not contain them.
The sands of time were running out,
  And we could not take it in -
She had cheated death so many times before.
 The grim harvester had called,
But she had said,
  Let me see just one more babe,
  Just one more wedding feast,
  Just one more venture bright
   Into western lands*
Where mountain and water meet, where otters play
  In the clear moonlight.
It is not time, said she, not yet.
But the sands of time were running out
  For the one we loved so much,
  And we could not contain them.

Had we known then what we know now,
We would have held her close.
  So close, so tight,
That he could not have cast his shadow
  Over her, nor touched her with his breath.
But we did not know the hour,
we could not understand the danger,
  And we let him in.

Teach us to number our days, O Lord,
  That we may not regret
   The chances missed
To sweeten the paths of those we love
With kindness, care and gentle words.

The intellect did grasp, for sure,
The meaning of the words "she died",

But not the heart.
Not the soul.
We were not prepared.

Like an onion,
The heart and soul
Have many layers.
Grief must penetrate,
And permeate,
Each one:
The consciousness, the semi-consciousness,
And then the deepest heart, the Great Subconscious.
Each layer must take it in,
Embrace, contain and own
The meaning of the words "she died".

The pain must be accepted by
These layers, one by one,
Sometimes a pain that sears, intense,
Sometimes a mere dull ache.

And in that recognition
The pain will come to be
A part of us.
Then will we be
Whole people once again.

* For our family, the west coast, the Highlands and Islands, have always held a deep attraction, possibly because our roots are there. For Olwen, a special trip to stay with her niece Ali near Ardnamurchan renewed her youth for another season, and to spend a night in Ali's campervan watching the otters playing by the seashore was a joy she had not expected to experience again in her life. It was a gift from God.

Dancing with Ghosts
(or "R" "U" Confused!)

This is the story of how the simple mis-reading of two letters of the alphabet led to half a century of mystery, a jig-saw puzzle of missing pieces, and confused identity for the daughter of a young Glasgow hero.

As Flight Lieutenant Ron McLean of the Dunblane Air Squadron rang the doorbell of the flat in Glasgow's West End, he wondered what kind of reception he would receive from the elderly lady living there. Part of the jigsaw was that her surname was the same as the maiden name of the widow he was trying to trace.

The mystery he was about to solve had started at 4.00 p.m. on Thursday, 28th September, 1944. Flight Lieutenant Duncan McCuaig had just successfully "shot" photographs of the Focke-Wolf factory in Bremen from his little, unarmed reconnaissance Spitfire, and was escaping as fast as he could with his vital information. Until the development of the newest Focke-Wolf plane, Germany had nothing as fast as the Spitfire. Not surprisingly therefore they didn't like these photographs being taken, and sent up two of their pilots to deal with the little British plane. The enemy planes, Focke-Wolf D-9s, came at Duncan straight out of the sun, and he didn't stand a chance. The German ace-pilot Robert Weiss scored another fatal hit, and the Spitfire plummeted to earth. Duncan baled out at 300 feet, pulling the ripcord of his parachute, but it failed to open, and seconds later he hit the ground. He was killed on impact, and his plane crashed into a field nearby, on a farm in the little village of Apelstedt, near Bassum, south of Bremen. Duncan was given a decent burial in the local graveyard, and his name marked on a simple cross. He was 24 years old when he died.

Under normal circumstances, his body would have been re-interred at the end of the war in a British Military War-Grave and the family would have been notified. The story would have been laid to rest along with the pilot.

However, at the time of transfer, possibly because of weathering of the original simple cross, or through human error, the name McCuaig was mis-read as McCraig. "R" and "U" confused!! The authorities could find no trace of a "McCraig" who had gone missing over Germany on that date, and in the confusion of war, the matter had to be left unresolved, with the pilot buried under a cross inscribed with the words "Unknown

Pilot" in the War Grave at Sage, near Oldenburg. Eventually his family assumed that he had gone down in the North Sea.

Another part of the jig-saw puzzle is the fact that Duncan McCuaig was married at this address in the West End of Glasgow, not in Killearn which was home for both of them. There is a treasured wedding photograph of the heart-wrenchingly handsome young R.A.F. pilot and his lovely bride. Olwen, named after an Irish princess, is as dark as Duncan is fair, and they are serenely and completely in love, and totally oblivious to the hardships of war. He was 21 years old, and she was 19. I imagine that they can scarcely believe that this second attempt at elopement has actually succeeded. The wedding has been clandestinely arranged with the connivance of her mother's cousin, Morag, a great ally! A cake has been baked with precious war-time rations begged and borrowed by Maria, the Polish refugee who lives in the basement flat; Great-Aunt Jessie's tiny-waisted wedding dress of gorgeous gros-grain silk has been brought down from the attic. During war-time, wedding banns needed to be displayed for just 24 hours, so that Duncan and Olwen had been in hiding for only one night, which they spent climbing Ben Lomond and watching the dawn. An excerpt from an old letter to his mother from Dr. Donald Girdwood, their best-man, explains how, in fear and trembling lest he should meet Olwen's father, he collected the marriage certificate. Her father had realized that he could do nothing to stop the marriage, so Donald also carried a letter of conciliation to Olwen: her parents attended the ceremony in Cousin Morag's drawing room, although her father was less than enthusiastic! They were married by the minister of Killearn Parish Church.

The newlyweds moved around a lot. As a reconnaissance pilot, flying solo in his tiny, unarmed Spitfire, Duncan took photographs that enabled the Army, Navy and Air Force to plan battle strategies. The Spitfire had to be unarmed because firstly the camera took up the space used by guns, and secondly, it had to fly fast to get in and out of enemy airspace.

They started married life in Cumbria at Silloth, then moved to Aberdeen, Bath, Bristol, Wick, Northern Ireland, Oxford, and Cornwall. When Duncan was stationed at St. Eval in Cornwall he would be flying on reconnaissance missions over France. From R.A.F. Benson in Oxfordshire, he flew out over Germany.

After a year, I was born. They were idyllically happy, deeply and spiritually in love. Only one great sadness had marred their lives: Duncan had only one brother, also an R.A.F. pilot: during the Dieppe landings

Duncan and Eric McCuaig

on August 19th, 1942, Eric had been shot down. He was picked up still alive in the English Channel but died on board ship and was buried at sea. I still cry when I think about the uncle I never met. Eric was a great charmer, very athletic, and with dark, curly hair, looking quite different to Duncan. He had been a promising actor and playwright when war broke out, and had won a scholarship to R.A.D.A., where his portrayal of Falstaff had been highly acclaimed.

In later life, Olwen reminisced about those days. She said that they didn't dwell on the fact that Duncan might not come home: it was a job to be done and they just got on with living.

I spent the first year of my life in a little house called "Boscarne", perched high on a Cornish cliff. The sound of the wind and the waves on the shore lulled me to sleep, along with the drone of planes overhead from nearby St. Eval airfield. In the evenings my parents sat and listened to the music of Sibelius and Beethoven and Brahms, talking of life after the war. They dreamed of moving to Loch Torridon where we had spent a holiday: there are photos of Duncan holding me as we row a boat together! Since I was only 21 months old at the time I guess my energy input did not add significantly to our progress!!

Shortly after that holiday, we were posted back to R.A.F. Benson in Oxfordshire. There is a photograph dated 17th September, 1944, my second birthday, with me sitting in my pram looking wistful, and the inscription beneath reads, "God bless Daddy, Daddy back soon." Well, sure enough, he did come back that day. Eleven days later, however, he failed to come back, and someone else in R.A.F. uniform came to the door to tell my mother the grim news that Duncan was "missing, presumed dead".

"Missing, presumed dead" is a ghastly verdict. The relatives cannot grieve properly as there is no body to bury: they hope against hope that their missing loved one will turn up some day. I picture my mother listening to every step on the gravel outside, watching the postman bring letters in the hope that there may be wonderful news, trying to calm the flutter of her heart every time the phone rang. Days went by, then weeks, then months, and still no news. Olwen and I moved back to a cottage along the lane from "Boscarne" where we three had been so very happy together. Perhaps she thought that if Duncan were to escape from a P.O.W. camp he might find his way back to this place of happy memories. Perhaps the surging sea and the soft Cornish air with its scent of tamarisk

Duncan, Olwen and Brenda

brought some element of healing to her breaking heart, but eventually she and I returned home to Scotland, where she planned to start a new life and become a writer.

Meanwhile another hero had returned home from the horrors of war in Europe, where he had led the flame-throwing tanks of the R.E.M.E. through France and Holland and into Germany. He was Major Douglas Drysdale, and he fell in love with Olwen, and, since all hope for Duncan was now gone, she married him and this wonderful man became my very dear step-father. (I was devastated when he died in 1984.) Olwen and Douglas gave me four brothers and a sister, and I had a very happy upbringing. People would tell me about Duncan, what a sweet person he had been, a dreamer, musical, very romantic, a bit impractical, and a fine mathematician and engineer; he was happiest in his old tweed jacket! It wasn't that my mother didn't talk about Duncan so much as that I think it was assumed that I remembered him too. After all, he had been there with us all the time. But the awful thing is that I can't remember him: he is just out of reach, like the sun behind a thick sea mist.

After my mother's re-marriage, first of all we lived near Killearn, moving soon to Glasgow. When I was 6, we moved to Dunblane, and six years later we moved to Dollar. Eventually I came to Glasgow to study. By this time my widowed Grandmother and my aunt had moved into the top flat of the old family house in the West End, with Cousin Morag occupying the lower flat. I went to live there, and at that time met my future husband, Ian Macdonald, who also had been an R.A.F. pilot. Another very romantic twist to the tale is that Ian proposed to me in the very room where my parents had been married 21 years previously, Cousin Morag's drawing room!

In due course I was married in Dollar to my own hero, Ian, by coincidence on *that* date, the 28th September, and we had four children. For 33 years I have been happily married, but nevertheless the spectre of unresolved grief haunted my early adult life, and I was troubled with recurring bouts of depressive illness, finally receiving help from psychotherapy. I discovered the healing power of writing, and part of a story I wrote was autobiographical: *"From that day onwards the young mother and her child waited and watched, waited and watched, and as the days went by, the young mother's heart slowly and steadily broke, and she wept and wept as she came to know that her handsome and brave young warrior was surely dead. And so the tiny child also learned about weeping. She*

Douglas Drysdale

who had known only laughter and love learned from early years about deep sadness. As time went by she forgot the sound of her beloved father's voice, the expressions on his face; his very features dimmed and faded altogether. But she had learned all about searching, searching, searching; looking into every face and personality for memories and fragments of the lost father whom she missed so very, very desperately. When she found a face, a voice, a personality that bore traces of that memory, she would love that person dearly. It seemed to be inevitable that many of these people had to move on out of her life, and her poor bruised heart would break again."

Meanwhile out in Germany, another piece of the jigsaw puzzle was taking shape. In the late 1960's a little boy called Werner was puzzled by the rows and rows of crosses in Sage War-grave near his home. He couldn't understand the concept of war at all. When he grew up he became an amateur war historian, and helped his friend Axel who was writing a biography of the German ace pilot, Robert Weiss, also known as "The Red Baron Of The Second World War", or "Bazi". Bazi Weiss's log showed that it was a Spitfire that he had shot down on 28th September 1944, but other records said that it was an American Thunderbolt. To verify the situation they went out with a metal detector, found the plane, excavated it, and confirmed that it was a Spitfire. The plane's number was still legible, and a local resident remembered what had happened that afternoon so long ago.

Werner contacted the British authorities to find out who the pilot had been. Had Werner not been a singularly caring and sensitive young man, he might have left it at that, but he wanted to let the pilot's family know the whole story, especially when the R.A.F, the Ministry of Defence, and the British Wargraves Commission seemed to have lost track of the family and did not know where Flight Lieutenant McCuaig had been buried. The only clue was that the former Mrs. McCuaig had remarried and moved to Dunblane.

Persistence is a virtue that Werner has in abundance, so he wrote to the minister of Dunblane Cathedral who could not help, but did suggest that the Dunblane Air Squadron might be able to help, since they were doing a project to find lost Spitfires for which Dunblane had originally raised funds during the war. With tremendous dedication and enthusiasm, Flight Lieutenant Ron McLean and his cadets undertook many hours of painstaking detective work: they cycled to Killearn to look at the War Memorial, and found the names of both Duncan and Eric

Duncan's Spitfire, with Olwen's logo.

Duncan climbing into Spitfire

there; then Ron drove to York to search the records of wills to see if any other family members were mentioned; and they searched the registrar's records, where they discovered that Olwen and Duncan had been married, not in Killearn Parish Church, but at a certain address in the West End of Glasgow. Failing to find any McCuaigs or Buchanans still in Killearn, Ron searched the telephone directory on the off-chance that he might find a Buchanan at the wedding address. When Olwen's sister answered the door that day, it was the breakthrough they had all been waiting for, and within hours I was told the news!

When my aunt came to the door of our little catering business, I was standing making tuna sandwiches. Somewhat hesitantly my aunt said to me, "Karen, I've just had some extraordinary news: they have found where your father's plane crashed in Germany."

It took a minute or two for the meaning of what she had just said to sink in. When it did, I felt as if I had been punched in the stomach. I remember gasping for breath. After 47½ years of "missing, presumed dead", this was dynamic news.

The next thing was to tell my mother. Olwen by this time was suffering from cancer of the spine, and right then was ill with flu in Strathcarron Hospice, who cared for her from time to time, although her home was in Dollar with my sister. I didn't know if she was going to be well enough to take this piece of news. The hospice arranged a room where we could be on our own, and I told her to a reaction of amazement, tears, wonder, laughter, more tears, and lots of questions. She made a rapid recovery from her flu, and once she was back in Dollar she had a visit from Ron McLean. Later that year, I went to the Dunblane Squadron's annual prizegiving where I received on her behalf a beautiful model of Duncan's Spitfire, PL 904, which stands on a little plinth with an actual part of the plane, and the following year she was well enough to present the cadets with a silver quaich to be given annually to the best photographer in the squadron.

The day Ron McLean walked into my shop and told me all about what Duncan had been doing, and the exploits which had earned him the D.F.C., I swear I grew an inch taller. I suddenly found an identity of my own. I had been proud to be connected to my lovely Drysdales, but that afternoon I became the daughter of a Spitfire Pilot, a hero to be proud of! It was as if one third of myself had been in shadow for all those years!

Meanwhile the R.A.F were trying to find Duncan's grave, but drew

Four generations - Olwen, Karen, Alison, Eilidh.

blanks everywhere they turned. Werner in Germany was doing detective work too, but nothing turned up. Gradually I absorbed the whole extraordinary story, and life returned to normal, with intermittent contact with Ron and his cadets to whom my mother and I felt a huge debt of gratitude. Their project on my father now included the information that "Bazi" Weiss had himself been shot down, three months after Duncan, by a Norwegian pilot called Karl Hannes, who died in 1970.

On Armistice Sunday, 1994, I was thinking about the whole story. As time had progressed with no news of Duncan's grave, Olwen and I both accepted that we would never know, but we felt content with the information we already had. The following day I arrived home from work to find a letter from The British Wargraves Commission telling me that they now had conclusive evidence of the whereabouts of my late father, and the day after that a letter came from the R.A.F. offering to fly me and my mother out to Germany for a memorial service at his grave.

In a telephone conversation the official from the Wargraves Commission explained to me that the papers relating to the "Unknown Pilot" showed that the misreading of "R" for "U" was quite unquestionably the origin of the 50-year-old mystery.

And how had the grave been found at last? Once again, my dear, persistent friend Werner had written another letter. On the fiftieth anniversary of Duncan's disappearance, 28th September, 1994, he had written to the British Embassy in Bonn requesting help. He had the strongest feeling about a certain grave at Sage, a grave marked "Unknown Pilot", and wanted further investigation carried out, hence the discovery of the confusion of "R" and "U".

Is it too far-fetched, I wonder, or biblically incorrect, to think that Duncan's spirit was restless because his beloved Olwen and Karen did not know his final burial place, especially in view of their spiritual closeness before his death? Could it be that Werner's gentle, emotional nature was sensitive to Duncan's restlessness, and that was the driving force which finally solved the mystery?

By the time the news reached us, Olwen's health was deteriorating badly, although she bravely planned to make the enormous effort it would have taken to go to Germany. We talked of the new gravestone which was to be placed almost immediately, and agreed that the wording should be "Now Rest in Peace".

Olwen never made it to Germany. She didn't need to: she and

Duncan and Douglas were united by death on 23rd December, 1994, and her funeral was the celebration of a wonderful life, lived with exceptional courage and faith, an inspiration to many other people. I felt immensely proud of her.

Olwen and Douglas were both very involved in the cause of Independence for Scotland, and at their funerals each had a wreath made in the likeness of the Scottish Flag, the Saltire. Duncan and Olwen had both been "exiled" to English boarding schools and Olwen maintained that Duncan too would have fought for this cause, being not so much anti-England as very pro-Scotland.

So now at last I will take a Saltire wreath to Germany for Duncan, and the R.A.F. will hold a simple memorial service. Being of a very romantic nature like my parents, it is my custom to lay a single red rose on the coffin of someone I have loved very dearly. There will be two red roses for Duncan, one from Olwen, and one from me. Entwined with the roses will be a piece of Cornish ivy, from in front of "Boscarne", the little house on the cliffs at Trenance. They will be tied with the other half of the red ribbon which tied the rose I placed on Olwen's coffin.

After fifty years, Duncan will now rest in peace, and I will give thanks for God's gift of the truth which has set me free.

You may wonder why I have called this story 'Dancing With Ghosts'. As I was writing it I cried buckets full of healing tears, while my whole self ached with longing to see my long-lost father and his older brother. At some point the radio was playing the haunting music of Sibelius' Valse Triste, and in my mind I was dancing with them, round and round and round in an endless, tragic waltz. My heart was nearly breaking and I felt that there was no escape from the pain. However, eventually God's promise in Isaiah 61: 1 prevailed, and His comfort reached through my pain and I cling firmly to the fact that I will see them again at my journey's end.

"The spirit of the Sovereign Lord is on me, because the Lord has anointed me to preach good news to the poor. He has sent me to bind up the broken-hearted, to proclaim freedom for the captives, and release from darkness for the prisoners, to proclaim the year of the Lord's favour, and the day of vengeance of our God, to comfort all who mourn, and provide for those who grieve in Zion – to bestow on them a crown of beauty instead of ashes, the oil of gladness instead of mourning, and a garment of praise instead of a spirit of despair." Isaiah 61: 1 – 3.

On the following page is the poem I wrote on my return from Germany after the memorial service.

Now Rest in Peace

Forgive me, please, I'm not quite here!
My body, my baggage
And part of my brain
Got up and got packed
And came home on the plane.

But my heart is not here:
It's there,
Beside my father's grave
Five hundred miles away.
Between my body and my heart
The North Sea lies.

In sandy German soil,
At Sage,
Nine hundred souls lie buried,
Heroes all.
Each one is known
Personally
To God;
Each one a story,
Just like ours,
Of life and love
And hope cut short
By war.

Each one a son,
And some were brothers,
Husbands, uncles
- fathers too.
Nearly all were young - just boys.

Sixty-nine are still "Unknown".
Their families,
Just like mine,
Have lived for years

With that grim news:
"Missing, death presumed."
They are amongst their comrades
In Sage's tree-lined peace.

I've seen it now
In summer sunshine
With rustling leaves
And gently cooing doves.
I must imagine frosty winter days,
The branches of the trees
White and glittering in the snow;
Or autumn's gales with driving rain;
Or springtime full of future hope.

The messages of love
On known comrades' graves,
And the perfume of *their* flowers
Must be sufficient.
Remembrance for all
Whose families just don't know.

Far from Scotland's hills and glens
This war-grave lies
On Germany's flat and fertile
Northern plain.
Red brick farms with pan-tiled roofs,
Bright flower-decked balconies,
And herds of cattle grazing
In lush green fields
Watered by slow, deep rivers rolling by,
The Hunte and the Weser:
A picture of prosperity and peace.

For me,
Five decades passed
Before I learned the truth.
And now at last

I've said farewell
With wreath and roses red
To the father
Whose memory so dear
Is imprinted in my deepest soul.
An ivy now is planted there
To let him know I've been
To see his final resting place.

A Guard of Honour
In Air-Force Blue
Attended.
The Last Post sounded
In solemn tribute,
The bugles shining bright.
A solitary piper played -
A Scot's lament -
While wreaths were laid.
The padre said a prayer.

Our German friend
Who found the truth
Linked hands with us.
We shed our tears
And asked The Lord
For peace on earth.

Suddenly a wind sprang up
And gusted,
Shaking trees and blowing leaves
As if in holy affirmation
That all is well.

With love from Karen

Duncan McCuaig.
Right, rowing at Loch Torridon with 21-month-old Karen

Ash Wednesday

Today is the First of March. Forty-eight years ago to the day, my mother married Douglas Drysdale, my beloved step-father, and today we will scatter her ashes beside the little trees where she scattered his ashes exactly ten years ago.

Dust to dust, ashes to ashes.

The sky is a bright, pale blue, full of the early promise of Spring. Trails of cloud drift across the landscape, some like smoke hanging mistily across the hillsides, some darker, laden with impending snow. The air is crystal clear, the lower mountains sprinkled lightly with snow and revealing every corrie and glen, the high mountains white and majestic in the distance.

I have allowed myself to be driven to Tullibardine by Alison and Douglas. Mairi, who has Mummy's names (Olwen Buchanan), is with us, and this is good. Little children with their innocent chatter keep things from becoming too melancholy. Eilidh, at five, would have found such proceedings too sensitive. Douglas is officiating, and has never been called on to do an ash-scattering ceremony before.

Forty-eight years ago the snow lay thickly on the ground. Today, the snow is only above the tree line, and there are signs of Spring. Ploughed fields add rich browns to the faded winter landscape, and there are even, quite unexpectedly on this high ground, some early lambs.

We reach Tullibardine Station House a little early, and park the car. Beside us a mass of snowdrops dance in the wind, and the tall pine trees sway on the steep slope of the railway embankment. The present owners are away, which they are sorry about because they would have welcomed us. Their little boy is gravely ill in hospital, and we grieve for them as we sit and wait. After a little while I get out of the car and go to investigate, (just in case the others are sitting waiting for us round at the other end of the house!!)

No-one else is in sight, and I walk further on. I drink in the sight of this dear, familiar place. Memories abound. The view is as breathtaking as it ever was, huge and wide, stretching all the way over the rich, fertile farms of Strathearn to the tree-dotted parklands around Crieff and the grandeur of the Grampian mountain ranges beyond. The near landscape is broken by dark green pine forests and little clumps of grey farm buildings here and there, and along the disused railway track, denuded of rails long since, are the familiar trees and bushes, birch and beech, oak and alder, rowan and hawthorn, that are home to birds of all kinds, and rabbits and squirrels, pheasants and stoats, and all sorts of little animals and insects. This place was a source of such peace and joy to Olwen and Douglas. I stand here and remember so vividly, as if it were yesterday.

As I walk further along the old platform, now covered in smooth, mossy grass, I am very glad of my warm coat, bought especially for Mummy's funeral. In spite of the brightness of the sky, the wind has a cutting edge, and the clump of Douglas Fir trees sighs and rustles. These are the trees which Mummy and Daddy planted so lovingly - how long ago? - must be sixteen or seventeen years ago!! The present owners have cut down one or two, but probably just to make space for the stronger ones to grow.

Oblivious of the cold wind and the solemn event taking place in the human world, some little birds are chirping and singing, and a flock of them wheel and circle over the fields, conscious only of the moment, and I wonder what they are finding up there.

My thoughts are interrupted by the arrival of Malcolm's car at the gates. He parks just outside, so I go to meet him, and when he gets out I give him a big hug. We don't need to say so, but we all miss her. Dreadfully. Together we walk back up the driveway, past the little chattering burn and the tall pine trees. Alison and Douglas are getting out of their car, with little Mairi, and we talk for a little, discussing the happy news that Douglas is to preach as sole nominee for Appin and Lismore parish, which means that he will almost certainly have the job! We take a good look at the Station House and talk about the changes that have taken place, and of which we all approve! We think that Olwen and Douglas would have approved them too, although Daddy's whole aim in life was always to have his cars safely garaged in the basement of his house, while the present owners have turned the basement garage into a centrally-heated study and office, a nicely-designed new double garage having been built elsewhere.

At this point Lorna and Bob arrive, with Sorcha, and with Mummy's ashes. Bruce opted not to come for his own private reasons. He spent much of his young childhood visiting his beloved grandparents in this house.

Mummy's ashes are in a brown paper parcel on which is written "The Late Mrs. Olwen Drysdale." Lorna unwraps the brown paper, and inside is a chocolate brown plastic jar, the size of a sweetie-jar. How odd, to be reduced to the contents of a chocolate brown sweetie-jar, I think to myself. Once more I am conscious of the sound of the wind in the tall pine trees.

The little family group wends its way up to the clump of trees on the old platform. A son, two daughters, a son-in-law, two grand-daughters, a grandson-in-law and a great grand-daughter. Bob knows the exact place where Mummy scattered Daddy's ashes. There used to be a group of three stones, and now there is only one, but it was on that same mound of earth, surrounded by the now sturdy little Douglas Fir trees. Unmistakable. We position ourselves round the place, Sorcha holding little Mairi in her arms, and Douglas holding The Ashes. And now Douglas is saying a prayer, simply talking to God quite naturally, and thanking Him for our Mummy and all that she was and did, her love for us all, her bravery and strength, her faith, her example. He commits her to God's care and peace as now we scatter her ashes to join those of her beloved husband. As he prays, little Mairi murmurs in her sweet child's voice, and Alison reaches to take her from Sorcha. Mummy would be happy to have a little child there, as would Daddy - they loved to have "wee people" around them.

Now Douglas turns to Lorna standing beside him and hands her the chocolate-brown sweetie-jar. She unscrews the lid, and leans forward to tip the light grey ashes onto the ground around the big stone. The wind rustles the trees, and somewhere a bird chirps. It seems to take ages to scatter all the contents around the rock. They seem very obvious on the ground, but strangely enough they don't blow away. I wonder to myself how long they will lie there before rain or snow soak the ground. I feel a tear roll down my face.

And so the deed is done. We walk slowly back to the cars, on the way stopping to have a closer look at the extension to the house and to admire how well it has been done.

Family tensions have to be forgotten just now, the solemnity of the proceedings bringing perspective to differences, albeit temporarily, and I remember that Mummy's final message to us all was that we should be comforted by our love for one another. I remember too that love never fails, that it perseveres and that it keeps no record of wrongs.

I am reminded that The Almighty has a sense of humour: today is Ash Wednesday.

Douglas (Dully) and Olwen's wedding

Au Revoir

(Until the Morning)

One by one
They slipped away,
Clara, Fiona, Graham,
Donald and Cam.
Exit stage right,
or maybe they left left (!),
Vitae dramatis personae –
These actors from the stage of life
On which we all perform.

One by one,
Silently,
They went,
Clara, Fiona, Graham,
Donald and Cam,
Vanishing offstage
Into the wings –
Those strange shadows
Of our imaginings.

If we could but understand
'tis we that lurk in Shadowland!

And what of them,
Our loved ones out of sight?
Why, now they play their part
On that much wider stage
Where dazzling light
Banishes
Tears
Forever,
And all that's left
Is joy
For them,
And here, for us,
The imprint of their lives
On ours.

With love from Karen

Sadly, over the course of December and January, we lost these five wonderful people.

First my very dear mother-in-law Clara to whom I owe so very much, who died thirteen days before her youngest grand-daughter's wedding. Then in January we lost my mother's sister Fiona, a very special auntie. Graham was a cousin, my uncle's brother, a dear quiet man whom we didn't know well enough but always wanted to get to know better. Then I heard the news of the death of my god-father in South Africa, Donald, a special link with my past. And last but not least, there was Cam, Dr. Cameron Macdonald, who guided me in adult years of depression through the pain of unresolved grief at the loss of my own father (missing, presumed dead, no funeral) when I was only a small child. Cam's skills as a psychotherapist and counsellor were God's gift in my life and thus indirectly to the life of my family.

Part Two

Moor and Mountain, Tree and Water

Summer Joy

Suddenly summer came!
Winter's icy grasp
Had clung tenaciously
Throughout the Spring,
Its persistent chill
Permeating even the slightest breeze
For months on end.
Grey clouds and rain had dampened
The merry month of May.
Summer however, like love at work
Upon the stubborn human heart,
Broke through: and now, the trees are ruffled
By the sun-warmed balmy wind.
The leaves hang thick and dark,
Richly green, the gardens full
Of rioting flowers and dancing blooms.
We fling the doors and windows wide
To let the summer in; and hoard the memory
Greedily
Against the shortening days' return.

With love from Karen

The Best is Yet to Come

Dedicated to Rev. H. Neil, to my parents-in-law, and to all the mature people who have helped me along the way.

While walking through the springtime woods
I think deep thoughts, and ponder:
Is this what Heaven's like?
Could it be lovelier than this?
Translucent veil of freshest green
Re-appearing over branches bare;
The hint of bluebell carpet spreading;
The birds are singing,
Pure and clear,
Warbling, chirping, trilling,
Filling the evening calm
With sweet, unblemished sound.

But no! A sudden commotion
Startles me. Two big, black rooks
Crash clumsily through bush and scrub,
And now I see the reason why:
Their dinner treat, a little squirrel,
Grey and cute and fluffy,
Is running for her life.
Just a baby, she ventured boldly forth
Not knowing what the dangers are,
And strayed too far.
Thankfully she gains the tree,
A sturdy beech,
And with the speed
Of wind through ripened barley
She ripples up the trunk
And scampers to the very top.

Watch out!! The big, black rooks
Have got there first!
So down she runs
And, quivering with fright,
Remains just where she is,
Halfway down the tree.
The human dilemma always is:
Whose side to take?
The squirrel's or the rooks'?
The cute or the glossy black?
The frightened or the hungry?
All are God's creation.
Heaven can't be like this;
Mortality has touched this place.

While lying on a summer beach
I think deep thoughts, and ponder:
Is this what Heaven's like?
Could it be lovelier than this?
The gentle tide is lapping
And swishing along the sand;
The distant mountains, blue and still;
A lark ascending into the cloudless sky
With liquid song;
The honey-scent of flowers
Filling all the air;
The turquoise sea glinting
And sparkling in the sun.
Sheer bliss!!

A peewit's warning cry
Rends the peace and quiet.
Some danger,
Man or beast unseen by me,
Has threatened
Her security.

Heaven can't be this:
Mortality has touched this place.

While walking autumn hillside
I think deep thoughts and ponder:
There surely is a hint of Heaven here.
The glory of these colours
Is beyond compare.
The mighty mountain's flank
Is clothed in purple, royal.
The forests and the woods
Are green and gold and red,
Russet, brown and dun.
The crags above are grey.
Reflected in the waters of
A distant loch,
The sky above is blue,
With touch of peach on sunset clouds.
The waters of the burn below
Are amber, peaty brown.
A falling yellow leaf
Reminds me:
Mortality has touched this place as well.

While walking through the winter woods
I think deep thoughts, and ponder:
What is Heaven like?
There is majestic power about this place:
The storm is tossing naked trees,
The wind is roaring
Through the snowy boughs,
Drowning the far-off city drone.
No other soul would roam outdoors in this!
The snow is whirling down
So fast and thick
I scarce can see my nose!

All is white,
Except some shiny evergreens
And dark grey trunks of trees.
But underfoot,
Beneath the snow and ice,
Lie dirt and death, the leaves
That once were full of fresh green life.
Mortality has touched this place.

What will Heaven be like, then?
Mortals will be there, for sure,
But not mortality!!
Mortals cleansed by Jesus' blood,
His mortality exchanged for ours!!

No tears,
No fears,
No hate,
No threat,
No sickness, aches or pain,
But all the love that we have known,
And more!
Complete security,
Acceptance,
Peace,
The promise of a body new!

The best of earth as we have known it
Is just a taste
Of what's in store.
THE BEST IS YET TO COME!!

With love from Karen

The Burn in Spate

for Kirsteen

Like life itself
it starts:
High up there
with God.
From the rocky heights
all white with snow,
it hurls itself
in foaming,
churning,
splashing
torrents,
tumbling
ever
down.

No gurgling, placid burn is this.
It crashes
headlong through
a wall of ice
and snow
on Corrie Clova's lip,
and mindless
of its proper course,
overflows its banks and full
of merry haste
falls
over itself
to get there
faster.

Its coffee, peaty, amber brown
is churned
and boiled
into a creamy white.
It rushes,

hastening down and down
in joyous glee.
Rushing,
roaring,
thundering past.
The boulders in its way
Rumble
and grumble
at its youthful haste.
Caring not, it tumbles
ever onwards,
down and down;
it never stops
to dream
in clear deep pools
of pebbled contemplation.

Not this burn!
No, it must get down,
and down some more,
and hurry on
to reach the glen,
and onwards fast
to reach at last
the restless, timeless sea.

Two mad March hares
in winter-white
stop gambolling
to watch.
They catch
the mood
and off they leap
and bound
through heather,
rock-strewn grass
and snow.
They chase and twist and turn,

climbing ever higher
till at last
they vanish
out of view.

Meanwhile
a caterpillar crawls
and clings to heather stem.
Optimism high,
it thinks the winter's past
and grabs the chance
to take a little sun.
Be not so hasty,
warn the walkers passing.
Look you up there and see
that wall of white above the corrie's lip,
that soft and swirling mist
even now is spilling
off the edge and downwards.
Stray you not too far
from rocky home,
or you may meet disaster.

The walkers scramble on,
and squelch
through heather, bog
and tufts of grass,
and scrunch then into knee-deep snow
which lies in melting patches
where the sun
glistens
on sparkling crystals.
On frozen Brandy's edge they sit,
three walkers tired and weary,
and gaze in awe at cliffs and rocks
and marvel at time's sculpture.

Loch Brandy, iced and still,
makes not a sound.

The wind is cold.
It's time to go,
so now that they are rested,
they downwards step,
or slither, slide and tread
with wary feet.
The conversation goes
on granite, schist and scree;
the glacier of aeons past
that shaped this place
and left its mark
for them to see.
They are but ants
in God's great scheme
for all eternity!

The houses look
like toys below;
the cars like bugs on ribbons
crawl
through patchwork fields
of brown and dun
and bright green winter corn.

So down they go,
the walkers three,
till they are in the glen
once more.
The burn is now a river deep,
still hastening on
to have
its great adventure.
Purposeful, mature,
it swirls and gurgles on its way.
It waters meadows,
pastures, fields.
The wooded glades are carpeted
with snowdrops,
pure and white.

On quiet crofts and farms
the evening smoke
curls upwards,
and the cattle graze,
contented.

The herald of the night appears,
the single evening star,
while the glowing sunset paints the sky
in colours rich.
The world is all awash
with gold-tipped rose
and fire-streaked peach,
while in the west
the clouds are touched,
the clouds from which
the angels make their wings.

And now at last
the walkers three
reach home
with weary limbs and sodden feet,
and filled with awe and wonder
at God's creation,
once again they know
His peace.

Still back out there
on hillside dark
the rushing burn in spate
keeps tumbling,
falling headlong down,
in moonlight clear and cold,
to reach at last
in joyous haste
the restless, timeless sea.

With love from Karen

Window Dreaming

I stand at the window
Surveying
My winter view.

Leaden clouds sweep in,
Gunmetal grey,
Lowering
With threat of rain
And storms to come.
Wind buffets at the house,
Windows rattle,
Trees moan in the woods,
While on wet roads
Car tyres swish.

I stand at the window
Watching.
A plane takes off
Down below,
A graceful silver bird
Shining white
Against the clouds.
Watching, I dream of places
That planes
Have taken me:
Places far away,
Transatlantic, exotic, hot,
Sometimes awe-inspiring,
Filled with fascination,
Steeped in history,
And nearly always
Wetter than
The natives said they should be!!

```
                steeply
        rises
The plane
```

Up, up and away.
It disappears
Out of sight
And into stormy clouds.

Out of *my* sight maybe,
But if I were on the plane
I'd see things
Differently.
For seconds only
The clouds are dark,
Then all at once
The sun is bright and I
Am in a magic land
Of blue and white,
Of fluffy valleys,
Billowy mountains,
Cloud oceans swirling
In gentle waves
To eternity.

(Is this what dying's like?
A swift transition
Upwards
To realms unseen
And unimagined?)

The cloudscape thins
And down below
A multicoloured quilt
Spreads out before my eyes.
Fields and moors,
Hills and sea,

Matchbox homes and farms,
Tiny ants for cars,
Trucks look more
Like fat black flies.

The plane flies
South or west,
Sometimes north or east
And leaves the known
Familiar land.
I've flown over
Myriad
Diverse works
Of our great God's creative hand.
Snow-capped mountains,
Volcanoes' fiery flow,
Sand-filled deserts,
Tundra grey and endless.
Mighty rivers carve the landscape,
And frozen lakes stretch out
For miles on end.
Forests of different shades of green
Hide things I cannot see.
Once I saw that awesome place,
That canyon gouged
Through the rocks of time itself
In Arizona's vast expanse.

Cities too,
Where man's creative talents
Have raised some wondrous things.
Mighty towers (of Babel?),
Homes for rich and poor alike
With gardens, parks and squares.
Palaces and slums,
Theatres, prisons and concert halls.
Cathedrals, castles and shopping malls
Temples unto Mammon!

Both East and West compete
In genius and ...inhumanity!!!!!

As I look down
On all below
I wonder,
Is this
How God views all His Earth?
What *does* He think
Of our funny stubborn ways?
How He must grieve
To perceive
Us getting it all wrong!
How He must long
To interfere
And *make* us
Get it right!

With love from Karen

The Pansies in the Garden and the Songbird in the tree

For Jean, my "best, best, best friend" --- friend of my youth

Once upon a time, Old Friend,
When we were still quite young,
We met upon the path of life
When it was just begun.

It seemed quite steep at times,
Though if truth were really known
'Twas really quite benign.
Learning stuff was what they said
That life was all about.
We didn't disagree with that
But thought that other things
Were
More exciting.
Like boys ....
Those beings of
The Opposite Sex
(shhhhhh!!!!!! We didn't even know
what that was all about!)

So while we studied
Maths and French
With Speedy, Jock and Cocky
Our minds (and hearts) were
Quite sidetracked,
And we couldn't see
The pansies in the garden or
The songbird in the tree.

After pastures green of early years
The 'Lower' slopes did beckon
And we shared the common burden

Of studying this path,
Going ever onwards
Till the ground got 'Higher'!!
And we didn't see
The pansies in the garden or
The songbird in the tree.

For rest and
Relaxation
We went, one day,
With bikes
To Stirling station!
In wind and rain we pedalled hard
And then we didn't see
The pansies in the garden or
The songbird in the tree.
All we saw was miles
And miles
And miles more miles
Of Skye!!

Then came the day
The pathway split.
Your path went east
While mine came west.
Higher, higher, up we climbed
And sometimes
On happy days
The pathways intertwined
And once again we shared
A few of all our cares and woes,
But mostly all our joys.

Our paths have been quite different
Yet, in many ways, the same,
With unexpected twists and turns,
Quite hidden from below,
That brought us treasures

That we never knew –
Treasures not foreseen
In the 'Lower' days of youth.

At times the path is rocky
And we may even need a rope
To haul us up when things
Get quite beyond our scope.
At other times the path is full
Of mud and dank, dark 'spooty bits'
That jeopardize
Our progress up the hill.

Then suddenly the sun
Breaks through
With a rainbow full of hope.
We turn around and look,
And see
The view of sixty years spread out below.
When first our paths did cross
We could not imagine that!
Once more our paths do meet,
And now, for you and me,
There's time to see,
The pansies in the garden and
The songbird in the tree!

With love from Karen on Jean's sixtieth birthday

Ode to my Leki

(for Catriona and Kirsteen)

I did it! I did it!
I bagged a Munro!
I got to the top
And far down below
The cars and the houses
Were smaller than mouses!
How quaint!

I did it! I did it!
I bagged a Munro!
And now I must tell you –
You've got to know!
Achieving at last
My impossible goal
Is really all thanks to
My wee Leki Pole!

1, 2, 3 a-Leki
4, 5, 6 a-Leki
7, 8, 9 a-Leki
Somehow I will get there!

It's new,
It's blue,
It's absolutely magic!
Without it
The consequence
Could be utterly tragic!

Moor and mountain,
Bogs and myrtle,
With legs like Ian's
I might hurtle!
But with legs like mine
I need divine

Intervention,
Not to mention
A block and tackle
Or a Leki!

1, 2, 3 a-Leki
4, 5, 6 a-Leki
7, 8, 9 a-Leki
Somehow I will get there!

When I was only forty-five
My get-up-and-go became alive,
So I bagged a Munro
And left it at that –
To climb any more
I had got too fat.
By the time that I was sixty-one
My get-up became
Completely undone!
But then they gave me
A Leki Pole –
They knew that without it
I would roll
All the way down
(If I'd ever got up!!)

So up I had to go!
So where was that Munro?
It's easy, said Ian,
Quite a doddle
Even if you
Can only waddle!

1, 2, 3 a-Leki
4, 5, 6 a-Leki
7, 8, 9 a-Leki
Somehow I will get there!

I gripped the Pole
With determination
And waded bravely
Through vegetation,
Heather, moss and spooty bits!
With a huff
And a puff,
Though blue in the face,
I tried to keep up with
Ian's great pace.
We're nearly there,
He said with glee!
We weren't!
The top had moved
To infinity!
(It always does!)

So onwards and upwards
We wearily climbed
Till all of a sudden
What did we find?
The cairn!! Hurray!
I did it! I did it!
I bagged a Munro!
That's two down now and only
Two hundred and eighty two to go!!

With love from Karen
After climbing Geal-Charn
At Drumochter

Walk in the Park
(November)

RED BERRIES,
Glowing,
Bright
Against the dark green holly leaves.
Christmas coming!
Red berries,
Glowing
On skeletal trees
Stripped bare of leaves
By last night's autumn gale.

The university clock
Chimes the quarter hour,
Slow, measured.
Ding. Dong.
Timeless time, calm and reassuring.
Students scurry studiously
Towards their classes.
Some stroll in pairs,
Heedless of the world,
Enchanted by the heady glow
Of youthful love.

A rook alights on treetop bare,
                    and caws.
A silver squirrel, leaf in mouth,
Ripples lithely up the tree
With mercurial speed,
The leaf to line his tree-top home -
All mod. cons., the view
                is quite superb!!
The swirling Kelvin flows below,
Gurgling and swift,
In spate with last night's rain.

The sun shines wanly, pale,
Behind a veil of thin high cloud,
But bright enough.
Christmas is coming!
There is an air
Of busyness and expectation. People
With things to do.

The grass is lightly frosted
And I can see my breath.
The paths are being brushed
To clear the drifts of autumn leaves
That fell last night.

An old man walks his Scottie dogs,
Slowly, shuffling through the leaves.
He sees the student lovers,
And, remembering his first love,
He smiles a fond, sad smile.
His first love, and his last -
She is no more.
They had their Spring,
And fruitful Summer years.
Then Autumn came.
And now he's in the Winter
Of his life.

But Christmas comes!
And with it Hope!
Red berries glow,
Bright against dark leaves!!

With love from Karen

Heat for Life

Standing in the shower,
Mug of coffee in my hand,
My senses revel in the heat.
Splashing water,
Like a hail of tiny hands,
Beating, pummelling, pounding
Hot comfort into weary joints and muscles tight!
The coffee warms inside from throat to toes
And soothes away my cares and woes!

The woody scent of curling smoke entices,
And draws me to the heat
Of red and orange embers.
Tongues of flame leap up
And heat me with their glow
On a frosty winter's night,
Banishing the numbing chill
From deep within my bones.

The heat of passion, surging through the veins,
Sets the very fibres of my being all aflame
With sweet desire
Which will not be denied
Until it's had its way.

We crave the heat of summer sun
While winter's snows are falling.
We think of sunlit beaches, sand and sea,
And dream of long cool drinks with ice.
But there is a heat which kills a man
Should he get lost
And wander in the sweltering desert sun.
That heat will scorch and parch
And finish him with fierce and fatal thirst.

In a furnace
Heat refines and purifies.
In white-hot, searing heat
All dross and filth are burned away
And all that's left is gold!

Heat, like life itself, presents us
With dichotomy.
We crave the comfort but eschew the pain.
One thing's for sure:
Without **heat**
We'd all be dead!

Sweet Heat

You want a poem about heat?
If I can do it, it will be a neat feat.

Heat rhymes with feet
But is spelled like sweat, not sweet.
(By the way, spelled
Can be spelled spelled,
Or, if you prefer,
It could be spelt spelt.)
Sweaty feet are not sweet.
Sweat is wet, not weat.
(Weat is what the English say for wheat, as in Weetabix,
While we Scots pronounce the "wh" like h - w, all soft!
Hweet!! ... Just thought I'd throw that in,
For good measure.)

Heat makes you hot,
Which I am not.
(At least, not right now.
In fact, very rarely,
In *my* house, but that's another story.)
If I want to be hot, that is, as in heated,
I need a sweater!!
No, no, that's not sweeter!
It's "swetter", as in wetter.
And that thing I plug into the wall,
That's a heater, not a "hetter".
(Is hetter anything to do with heter-o-sexual, I ask myself.
Don't worry, myself didn't answer. Myself is too cold!)

Hot heat makes sweaty feet which are sweeter than ...
What?
(Or "wot?", if you are English. We Scots say "hwat?"!!)
Is it neat to have sweet sweat?
Is it a neat feat to have sweet sweaty feet?

You need heat to have sweet sweat in a sweater with a
heater.

And so ends my tale of heat.
That is "tale", spelled t-a-l-e.
The other kind of tale is "tail", spelled "t-a-i-l",
And that means the same as "end",
Except that I can't write, "And so tails my tale of heat!"
That would be rubbish!!

So what's the rest, you ask!!!

Narrow-Boat Reflections

In the spring of 1999 we joined Ian's cousin Keith for a delightful adventure on a narrow-boat named Bilbo Baggins on the English canal system. This was my 'word-picture' of the event, recorded as a thank-you to Keith, without whose dream it wouldn't have happened.

MAY

Black and white, fresh-painted, the lock gates
Beckon Bilbo Baggins on.
Up, up and up, the Hatton Flight ascends.
The windlass turns the paddle, the water rushes
Swirling, gurgling, through the musty smelling space.
The lock drains out, Bilbo Baggins edges in,
The crew, with heave and shove, push the solid wooden gates
Then turn the paddles once again,
Till the water pours back in, a swishing, tumbling froth.
Inch by inch the narrow-boat climbs up, and the helmsman
sees,
Like the next page in a book,
The view appearing.

Lock-keepers' cottages, with gardens neat and tidy,
Villages, with houses quaint and pubs with friendly welcome,
Towns with wharves and boatyards,
Warehouses, factories, cathedrals and spires,
Fields with cows - the smell is quite unique -
Meadows with sheep and pastures with horses,
Country mansions with sweeping lawns and spreading trees,
All slide past, a tranquil kaleidoscope of rural English peace.

Weeping willows trail their branches in the water,
Bowing low to see their mirror image.
Trees of every shade of green,
Vibrant with summer's early promise, sigh and rustle
As we round a bend to find

The perfect mooring place at end of day.
Sweet smelling woodsmoke, curling lazily
From Bilbo Baggins' chimneypot, tells of cosy warmth within
And tasty supper cooking to feed the hungry crew.
Who knows what delicacy awaits tonight?
One of Karen's Culinary Concoctions
or a spicy Curry À La Keith?
Stomachs are fed and conversation flows,
The debate becomes quite spicy too!!

Meanwhile outside, the evening air is filled
With birdsong sweet and pure. One owl cries to another,
To-wit, to-woo, while in the distant woods a cuckoo calls.
The archway of the red brick bridge
Reflecting in the waters of the old canal below
Remembers history long since gone,
The days when boats like ours
Carried the very lifeblood of England's industry.

The morning sun awakens us, sending shafts of dappled light
Across the golden panelled wood above our bed.
Reflections of rippling water, ruffled by the wind
That sighs through leaves outside.
Through curtains closed across leaded windows
Blue skies beckon. The bed rocks gently as the current flows
Against ropes now taut, now slack.
The sounds of the canal assault our ears:
The trilling birdsong just above; the gravelly scrunch
As Bilbo's bottom rubs along the ground below;
the cat-like purring
Of a two-stroke somewhere near.
Get up! Get dressed! Get ship-shape! The day's begun!
Coffee! Toast! And plans for where we'll go today.
A thrumming roar, and Bilbo's engine springs to life,
Insistent and compelling, his heartbeat drives us on.

One solitary heron stands, watchful, on the bank,

His reflection in the water ruffled
by Bilbo Baggins' gentle wash.
He waits just long enough for me to get my camera
And then takes off, flapping his wings with graceful ease,
Retreating to safe distance.

A duck and drake swim by,
eight ducklings following obediently behind,
Bobbing like weightless balls of floating fluff.
Another drake comes by, preening his feathers bright,
Metallic blue-green plumage shimmering in the sun.
Bilbo sails a bit too close!
The drake takes off with raucous quack,
His head head bent low, he squawks a time or two,
And then with feet stuck out below
He crash lands, skidding through the water
With expertise, a few yards further on!
A swan sits on her massive pile of sticks
And waits serenely for her eggs to hatch,
Her faithful mate nearby.
And look! A moorhen watches as we glide by
From the safety of the nest she's built that clings
Precariously amidst the rushing waters of a weir!
Bilbo Baggins chugs on by,
the engine puttering with peaceful purpose.
We sail through banks of creamy lace,
The honeyed scent of hawthorn and acid-yellow rape.
The flowers abound: buttercups and iris,
Forget-me-not and periwinkle blue,
Comfrey and ragged-robbin, and many more.

And so on, down to Stratford whose intellectual charm
Is quite a change from country life
With its funny little ways (like Plumbing Conservation!!)
An evening at the theatre, to hear and see
The tale of Oroonoko's plight.
Ancient houses thatched in reed,
And steeped in history. Some shopping too - a pair of shoes,

Some food, a book on Bilbo Baggins' name.
To finish all, a gourmet meal -
Fish and chips off paper in the park!!
Down Avon, into Severn,
Swift flowing, broader waters, with great weirs and locks
and craft galore.
Then into Worcester's city. The joyful peal of bells rings out!
Hot air balloons go sailing by, a rowing team,
A dragon boat, a coracle as well!
A hungry swan pecks Bilbo Baggins' paint!

Every scene enchants!
I want to keep and hold each fascinating impression.
And now we've shut the last lock gate,
And moored at Wolverhamption, Bridge 61.
I treasure every memory.
I may not pass this way again.

With love from Karen

Part Three

Big Issues

God Is Dead

"God is dead",
The people said.
They'd killed Him yesterday:
They'd taken Him down
To the end of the town
And nailed Him to a tree.

"God is dead",
The people said,
"We'll do our *own* thing now.
The human race
Has come of age.
We'll solve the problems now.
We have invented Science,
And the Media,
Not to mention Sex.
(Perhaps that's where
We did go wrong:
We mentioned Sex.
But never mind,
We'll make it Safe,
And then we'll be All Right.)
Self-fulfilment,
That's the thing!!
If it feels good,
Do it."

"Who is God?"
Our children asked.
And we replied
That He
Was a quaint,
Old-fashioned notion
Thought up
By people long ago,

The answer to
A primitive need,
No science there at all!

Jesus watched,
And wept.
His hands were sore,
His side and feet throbbed too.
At length He spoke.
"Father," he said,
"There's none so blind
As those who will not see.
Forgive them," He asked,
"For they know not what they do."

With love and sadness from Karen

Dunblane

In Dunblane.
Sixteen.
Children.
Dead.
And their teacher.
The gunman
has shot himself
as well.
The town is in a state of shock.
The nation too is stunned
at the enormity
of the massacre.

Sixteen, dear God.
Not one.
Not two.
But *sixteen*.
We cannot grasp this number.

And *children* too. Dear God,
help us to comphrehend
what we are hearing.
Not terrorists.
Not soldiers.
Not even pensioners
with lives fulfilled.
But little children,
innocent.

And in *Dunblane.*
Not in Belfast.
Not in Bosnia.
Not in some far-flung place
of war and strife,
but here at home
in Scotland.
Not in some drug-racked city slum,
not in a violent place,
but in Dunblane,
cathedral city,
country town -
the town where I grew up -
community of fellow Scots
going about their daily work,
in peace.

We sit and listen,
quite appalled,
to the oft-repeated news.
The story grim
unfolds
so many times a day
and every time we are compelled
to hear it all,
again,
as if by hearing
we can share -
somehow alleviate -
the burden of the grief
they bear,
those parents who
have lost
a precious, precious child.

In Dunblane we saw
the very worst
of man's inhumanity to man,
and yet, as one reporter said,
the very best was shown too
of man's compassion, strength and love.

And the gunman,
what of him?
What depths of pain
had seared his soul,
and caused
this gross
depravity?
How did society
hurt him,
that he must seek revenge
so black?
To what awesome depths
of loneliness and hurt,
rejection,
and loss of self-esteem
did he descend - the very pit
of Hell itself -
that Satan could
possess his soul
and wreak this evil deed?
Society - that's me, and you -
what could *we* have done,
you, or I, or anyone?

The Bible says, "Forgive",
but that's a notion
far too hard,
almost quite obscene.
Dear God, all we can ask just now
is that You
will pour Your comfort
on these families overwhelmed
by grief;
that You will grant them
courage to survive
the days, and weeks, and months
of bereavement's bitter torment
and anguished sorrow.
Grant them, we pray,
the grace, as time goes by,
to find acceptance of this deed
and so at last some solace in
their time of desperate need.

Again and Again

This poem by Frances Ennis was published in the MILNGAVIE & BEARSDEN HERALD, 30 October 1998

Remind me, again
why this world is so cruel
why there are laws
when we break every rule

Remind me, again
why this world is unjust
why the people we love
are the ones we can't trust

Remind me, again
why we can't live in peace
why our continual wars
don't ever cease

Remind me, again
why we are killing our race
why we don't have the love
and we can't find the grace

Remind me, again
of the respect I am due
and the respect I don't get
because I am different from you.

Answer to Again and Again

This reply was published in the Milngavie & Bearsden Herald, *20 November, 1998*

I'll remind you, again,
Why this world is so cruel:
It's the people who live here,
Our sin breaks the rule.

I'll remind you, again,
Why this world is unjust:
We're rotten and selfish;
The cost is too great
    when we're open to trust.

I'll remind you, again,
That we can't live in peace
'Cos we want, in our greed,
Lots of things to replace
Our spiritual need.

I'll remind you, again,
Why we kill and don't love:
We got so full of self,
We forgot all about God.

I'll remind you, again,
That He loved us to death;
He even forgave us
With His last dying breath.

I'll remind you, again,
That He loves every race,
And, to get on with each other,
He gives us all grace.

I'll remind you, again,
Of respect that He's due.
Just give Him first place
And He'll change things for you.

The Cancer-Spectre
(for my family)

*[The day after this was written, I saw the Senior Consultant
who gave me the ALL CLEAR!!]*

The cancer-spectre called this week.
With fingers long
and greedy
she caressed my breast.
There's something there,
The doctor said,
I'll need
to do
a needle-test.

The week before,
I spoke to God.
If by my dying, Lord,
I said,
my children could but know You,
then I am willing.
So I said, and shrank with fear,
but having said,
I meant it.

And now I think,
and think some more.
My mother's dead,
my fathers both as well.
Has my turn come so soon?
I am not ready,
No, not yet,
My house is too untidy.
My affairs are such a mess!
My best beloved needs
His wife,
Who chatters like a babbling brook
And shuts out other noises!

My children need
Their mother too,
Someone to love and spoil them.

I told the cancer-spectre,
I'll fight you all the way.
I know, she said,
That's why
I challenged you today.

Said I,
I'll fight, and fight,
With God's full armour shining bright.
I'll beat you back!
You shall not get your way!
And then my children
and my sister too
need fear
your threats
no longer.

The other spectres of old age
retreated
respectfully.
The spectre of
the creaky joints,
his fellow of the
wandered mind,
the others with their aches and pains
and failing faculties,
seemed strangely ineffectual.
I had thought to have their company,
and feared
for years of misery.
But now I contemplate
the other,
shorter
route
to better things: the promise
of a body new.

The best is yet to come,
preached he
whose worthy years
have given food for thought.

But what is death,
this journey
to another land
where body new
meets those
who went before?

Who says we must
grow very old
and stiff,
and "lose the place"?
Perhaps there is
this shorter route,
the cancer-spectre's way.

But no,
I do not bow
to a reign of fear
and dread.
But rather, I accept
the way
planned out for me
by the loving Father who,
in wisdom far beyond
my comprehension,
gives peace,
and all I need
to see me through,
whatever may befall me.

With love from Karen

Hope

My eternal thanks go to God for giving me a husband who stood by me, despairing but ever patient during several spells of this misery, and a sister who gave me support and understood some of what God was trying to get through to me.

The depression-spectre
sidles in,
unobserved,
and wraps herself around me
like a dull, grey fog.
She pervades my very being
and robs me of the will
to think, or do, or be.

She stills my laughter
and fills me full
of groundless fears.
She even quells
the healing flow of tears.
I want to cry,
but cannot. I am so tired.
I cannot think, I cannot feel,
I cannot love.

There is a pain, I know not where.
Like drowning man I reach
for spar of wood
in storm-tossed sea,
but reaching out
find nothing.
I would die, but cannot.
A vague foreboding fills me
all the time: grey dread

lurks there beyond
the far horizon.
The sunniest day is seen
through smoked-glass lenses.
My God, My God,
I cry,
have You deserted me?
[Now, years later, I know
that He did not.]

This is the soul's dark night.
A desert
experience.

But here is hopeful thought
from one who's been there.
In nature's plan comes winter;
dark, short days
and even darker nights;
branches stripped of leaves,
and not a flower in sight;
snow and ice,
then wind and rain;
frozen pipes,
then water, water everywhere,
sodden carpets, ruined homes,
illness, colds and flu.

It's now, beneath the wet, brown earth
piled up with leaves and snow,
that a miracle occurs.
A tiny, dormant snowdrop bulb
puts out its roots
and starts to feed.
For many months it lay there, fallow,
just resting from its effort

in darkness,
visited perhaps by worms.
So too the acorn
which last year fell,
and separated from its tree
starts life anew,
a brand new entity:
it too lies in the dark
and gains its sustenance
far from the joyous light of day.

The God whom many see
as "non-sense",
and therefore disbelieve,
believes in us
regardless of our disbelief.
He gave us talents at our birth
and on
the Day of Reckoning
asks us
for an accounting -
not for the talents He did not give
but for those
He did.
Now, like the tiny acorn
is the talent,
and in the soul's dark night
of winter bleak
the talent grows
and puts out roots
and shoots.
If in human things
these roots should grow,
the outlook is
but chancy;
for human things are
transient: can die,
reject
or turn to hate.

In God alone
can roots take hold
with any certainty.
Perhaps we know Him not,
and trust Him even less.
But He has given promises
that can, and should, be tried.
This Creator-God above
has made us in His image so
that we are not fulfilled
till we create as well.
Our "acorn-talent" may be planted
where we did plan
in blind attempt to make our mark.
but as in nature, sometimes,
a squirrel or a bird will move
our bulbs and seeds,
and they will grow
elsewhere,
so God does with our lives.

We plan our way in one direction,
but somehow things go wrong.
Perhaps we try some other thing,
but it's not too long before
we're in a mess.
The depression-spectre sidles in,
silently.

It's not until
we find
that talent
hid by depression's gloom,
the soil of God's bleak winter,
and humbly seeking guidance
start to use it,

that, bit by bit,
the winter's chill, depression's thrall,
will start to fade.
The snowdrop blooms,
the acorn sprouts,
the buds grow green,
the sun comes out,
and, gradually receding,
the greyness goes
and in its place
Spring once more appears.

With love from Karen

The Big Issue

I

Come from
A sheltered place,
Warm, secure and loving -
Middle-class, they call it.
My family "good",
My education was the best.
Now neither rich, nor poor,
But with a wealth
The bank can't count or store.

And yet I feel
Humble
In the company
Of my Big Issue seller.
He, so thin and drawn,
Somehow,
I don't know why,
Puts me to shame.

His name -
We'll call him Joe -
The same
As my own son, his age as well.
There but for God's good grace
Goes any one of us.
We're a' Jock Tamson's bairns.

Joe's face is tired,
He's thin and cold,
His back is sore
And he must stand for hours.
He knows things
I've never known,
And he's only half my age.

I would like to give.
But what?
People warn and tell me
I'm naïve.
"You'll get taken for a ride," they say.
So what to do?

Dear God, you said,
"Give unto the least of one of these
And you give unto me."
But what to give?

I'd like to give a carpet
For Joe's new flat.
That would be nice!
But my old carpet's worn and bald!!
Or how about some curtains?
That's a laugh!
Mine are tattered with many years of use.
So what to give?

I'll give a smile,
My friendship warm,
And prayers.
I could maybe bake a cake!
Or buy for Joe
A pair of woolly socks
To thaw his frozen toes.

But there are other Joes out there,
And starving children too,
Victims of flood and quake,
Hurricane, war and drought,
People with no food,
Babies dying, helpless.
Little children with enormous eyes
Looking to us
For help.

Intolerable pain.
And the politicians slaughter sheep
And bury them unused.
Dear God,
What can I do?
Where should I start.

The issue is too big for me,
So I'll just buy Joe some socks.

With love and sadness from Karen, after the slaughter of sheep and goats with 'scrapie' following new Government legislation.

Help!

Written after a visit to my lovely Auntie Brenda

My soul is screaming out
In pain.
Yesterday
I was in a perfect place.
I woke up in a peaceful room,
I looked out at lovely gardens,
I breathed fresh, spring air
And heard the sea upon the shore.
All around me there was order,
Beauty, simplicity, tidiness, symmetry.
Perfection. Serenity. Peace.
A haven for my soul, a taste of Heaven.

All day I travelled,
Surrounded on all sides
By evidence of God's creative genius.
Mountain grandeur, snow-capped peaks,
Range on range of soaring crags,
Draped in swathes of mist,
Or fading into deep-blue grey,
The enigmatic yonder.

I journeyed on by sparkling lochs,
Up over moorland brown with winter still,
Shades of dun and straw, khaki, faded gold
And glowing russet where the bracken
Lay soaked with last week's rain.
Then onwards,

Past forests green and woods
Whose trees are fat with unfurled leaves,
And pastures full of sheep
About to have their lambs;
Banks gloriously yellow
With gorse, daffodils dancing
And pale primroses peeking;
Birds singing and rivers rushing by,
Swollen with melted snow.

All the while my soul rejoiced
To see the wonder of it all.

But now, today,
I am back home.
Chaos clamours noisily around me,
Disorder, clutter, the tyranny of things.
A raucous and discordant cacophany
Of possessions stacked in crazy piles,
All stridently demanding
My attention, ravenously devouring
All the joy
From deep within my soul.

I long to live - to *be* -
In a place of tranquility such
As I have left just yesterday.
How can I get free?
How to rid myself of *things*?
Books - many still to read,
And some to keep and treasure;
Letters - must answer those!
Then put in pile for filing!!
Junk mail - might be useful one day,
(You never know!!)

Photos - can't bear to part with *them*!
Magazines - full of helpful trivia,
Not to mention recipes
Which I might try
(When I'm not On A Diet).
Begging letters from charities: well,
I've spent
All my money for the next two months,
But maybe, after that, I might consider
A small donation.
Pot plants - well, I can't bin them,
They're *living* things. Mind you,
They're nearly dead because
I should have watered them a month ago,
But didn't: they got lost
Beneath that pyramid
Of newspapers which aren't my mess at all,
But Ian's!!
And see those cardboard boxes!! No,
I simply can't remember
What's in them, if anything at all, but,
If they're empty,
They might be
Useful.
That carton of empty bottles in the porch
Could go - if I had time -
To the bottle bank. I'll do that when
I'm taking all those clothes
To Oxfam. Or, should I
Take them to a better cause maybe?
The Cancer Shop perhaps?
Maybe I should keep the clothes in case
One day I might get slim and fit them.

So many Things to care for,

And over each a layer
Of dust
Which I don't have time to clear
Because I'm busy shopping
For more Things!

Sure, I can laugh at Me,
But I'm not sure
If I can live with Me.
My soul
Is screaming out
In pain.

With love from Karen

Trapped

Trapped, I am.
Trapped.
Imprisoned.
Incarcerated.
Caged.

Trapped
By circumstances
Beyond
_My_ control.
I want out.

But My God says,
"You shall know
The Truth,
And The Truth
Shall set you
Free."

Trapped and caged,
Incarcerated,
Imprisoned.
This is not what I had planned.
Not at all.
I did not plan
To be engulfed
By bone-crushing weariness
Nor to be
At the constant mercy
Of other people's demands
For food.

I asked for
Freedom
To enjoy
Creation,
The flowers and trees,
The scents and sounds,
The wind, the rain, the breeze.

But Jesus said,
"I am The Way,
The Truth,
And The Life.
You shall know The Truth,
And The Truth shall set you
Free."

How can this be?, I ask.
When I prayed for time to dream,
To be with friends and family,
To make my house a home,
You, my Lord and God,
Said, "No!
Not yet.
All in *my* good time.
Come unto *me*, you who are weary,
And *I* will give you rest.

Take *my* yoke upon you
And learn from *me*,
For I am gentle and humble in heart,
And you will find rest for your soul.
My yoke is easy,
And *my* burden is light."
(Matt. 12:23)

And then I did begin to see.
Why should *my* lot be
Much less
Than theirs
Who have to bear
The care of parents frail and old,
Or children sick
Or blind or deaf or lame?
Or those whose lot it is
To have no job,
No home,
No dignity?
Is my prison not
An easier place to be?

And so, dear God,
I come to you
And ask you please to give
A willing spirit
And a change of heart,
The grace to say
With all my soul,
"*Thy* will be done, not mine."

And now I claim your promise, God,
Which in your Word I found:
Do you not know?
Have you not heard?
The Lord is the everlasting God,
The Creator
Of the ends of the earth.
He will not grow tired
Or weary, and His understanding
No-one can fathom.

He gives strength to the weary
And increases the power
Of the weak. Even youths grow
Tired and weary, and young men
Stumble and fall; but those who hope
In the Lord will renew their strength.
THEY WILL SOAR ON WINGS
LIKE EAGLES; they will run and not
Grow weary; they will walk
And not be faint.
(Isaiah 40:28-31)

With love from Karen

This and the following one were written at the time when we had been in business working a 90-hour week for 3½ years. It was an experience I wouldn't have missed for anything, but I was totally exhausted and desperate to find a buyer so that we could retire and I could spend time with my mother and my family.

Ode to a Lady Lawyer

Today
I am in a nightmare.
The tension
grips
my mind,
In my body
every muscle,
taut
as an overstretched
violin string,
shrieks
with raucous discord.

A nightmare ends
on waking up.
Not so this situation.
One's whole life
hangs
in the balance
of another's judgement.
I am caught in time,
in a moment
which lasts
for seeming eternity.
I do not know
the outcome
of the lady lawyer's judgement.
She is playing games
with people's lives,
and all she knows
is her own cleverness.

She does not care,
or even know,
about my shrieking nerves,
intent as she is

on scoring
clever points.

My life
for this nightmare time
is like an autumn leaf.
Ripped off my parent tree,
my source of succour
and strength,
by the sudden gale
of someone else's whim,
I lurch and tumble,
I am caught and thrown high
then tossed around
and dashed harshly
to the ground.
I know not where
my final resting place
will be,
but on the way
I am battered,
bruised
and soiled with mud.
The gale
has torn me
to shreds,
and, like the lady lawyer,
cares not a jot.

Madam,
if children suckled
at your breast,
one wonders, was it
vinegar they drank,
not milk? - you,
the woman who
annihilates
with clever wits

all shreds of
honesty,
integrity,
generosity
and trust.
You render worthless
all our hours of toil,
the business
we have built.
You make us out to be
common criminals,
and then go home
and sleep.

We,
meanwhile,
are poised,
alert,
nerves jangled by every "tring"
of the jarring telephone.
What does *our*
future hold?
Only you,
Madam Lawyer,
have the
power
to fulfil our dreams.
You -
and God.

Written in absolute despair
With love from Karen

When we were in the process of selling a business, and the
buyer's lawyer was using stalling tactics. We later discovered
that it was not because she didn't trust us, rather that she
suspected that he was not up to running this business! All we
wanted was to retire, and I had visions of working 90 hours a
week until I was 94!!

The Church

Deserted, neglected, shabby, forlorn. The little red sandstone church stands sadly on the corner. Once it was a haven of peace where tired and weary souls could come and pray or seek the solace of some comforting words from the parish minister, but for many years now the tenancy of this dusty and grimy place has belonged to the pigeons who happily nested and perched on roof and rafter, window-ledge, beam and bell tower.

Once the rafters rang with music, the joyful sounds of the organ pouring out praise and worship to a God whom the congregation knew and respected and loved, a heavenly Father to whom they turned for everything, to whom they sang of happiness when children were born, to whom they consecrated those children soon afterwards, before whom they solemnly vowed faithfulness when they grew up and confirmed the promises made on their behalf. It was here that the congregation gathered when a man and a woman undertook to love, honour and obey each other in marriage until death did them part, and it was here that they came, when, in the awesome and mysterious face of that death which did part them, they sought the security of committing their loved ones into the eternal care of this same God.

In ancient times, when the Canaanites lived in the Middle East, they worshipped a god called Moloch. Moloch was a hungry, angry god, and his uncertain temper could best be placated by a sacrifice of burnt baby. Hard as it is to believe, these tragic people truly believed that they were doing the best thing possible by regularly consigning their newborn children to the flames in ritual sacrifice. Moloch is still alive and well, and in fact he is even hungrier and angrier than ever. We don't call him Moloch any more, however. One of his names is Jones - he and his wife are the people we try to keep up with, remember? Well, he's just Moloch in a business-suit with a mobile phone. The desperate tragedy of our times is that, just as surely as the ancient Canaanites gave their children to the flames of Moloch, we are doing the same. Instead of ritual sacrifice by burning, we have permissiveness, promiscuity, pornography, abortion, drugs, unemployment, the total breakdown of family life through infidelity, divorce and broken relationships, and along with all these, the confusion of syncretism. The volatile god of this world is hard to placate, and increasingly demanding and unpredictable. The society that stands for nothing falls for anything.

Because of Jones and his little ways, we no longer need our little red sandstone church. No one has been there for a very long time, and indeed people have forgotten what to do when they get there.

One day the digger comes. Loaded onto a huge transporter it arrives, negotiating the corner with enormous difficulty. The little church watches, and its timbers shiver in dreadful anticipation, much like I do before I visit the dentist, imagining each stab of searing pain even before the operation begins.

The digger rolls forward on its caterpillar tracks, stops as if to draw breath, and then, rearing up like some prehistoric monster, lunges out and with its scoop greedily munches a chunk of the gable end, while the church crumbles before its aggressor with the same air of dignity, weary and silent, that so marked the last hours of the carpenter from Nazareth whose followers built this little church some nineteen hundred years later. "Father, forgive them, for they know not what they do", said the man from Nazareth, and his Father looks at what mankind is doing to himself in his haste to progress, and He grieves for His children who have so misunderstood His intentions, though He knew right at the beginning that they would. The demolition men pull down the far end of the building first and, after removing the valuable stone and stacking it at the far end, they pile the rubble up high in the centre of the building and drive the digger on its big caterpillar tracks up onto the mound of rubble so that they can attack the spire.

Now it is 6 o'clock on a cold, clear autumn morning. Against a chill navy blue sky spangled with sparkling white stars the broken remains of the church tower stand, washed in the cool white light of the crescent moon which hangs behind it. Its crumbling dark outline defiantly stands its ground (for a few more hours at least), face to face with the aggressor, which at the moment is at rest with its jib bowed low and its cab wrapped over in polythene sheeting and ropes to keep it from the inquisitive fingers of vandals.

Later, on the sunny afternoon of the same autumn day, a curious fact begins to make itself apparent: now that the building of the church has been removed, the light of the sun is reaching places it never reached while the building itself was there. Could it be that God is saying that we have spent too much time on the buildings with all their expensive and time-consuming maintenance, that they have become a stumbling block to us building a church of people, where *we* are the stone and the mortar, the windows, the doors, the paintings, the heating, the lighting, the floor, the roof, the very fabric of the "church"? In our well-intentioned attempts to glorify God by building beautiful churches filled with some of mankind's greatest expressions of (God-given) creative talent have we not got ourselves sidetracked into the need to spend money keeping these wonderful places warm and dry and in good repair at the cost of neglecting our brothers and sisters and failing to let them know about God?

The well-intentioned lady who cried out "sacrilege, sacrilege" and quoted scripture at the demolition men because they were pulling down the church on Sunday might have got nearer showing them the love of God if she had taken them a cup of tea and a scone.

Maybe those same men are hurting badly inside, yet they don't want to know a God whose followers are critical and self-righteous. Maybe they don't know how to love their wives and children, and maybe they hide from life in a smoke-filled pub in an alcoholic haze while their wives run off with other men and their children shoplift and joyride in cars and take drugs because no-one cares. Maybe it's time that the Christians saw the sacrilege in their own lives as they sit smugly in the declining number of churches while their unsaved brothers and sisters tumble headlong into the flames of eternal damnation that starts in the here-and-now.

Several weeks later a huge mound of rubble lies there untouched. Stone, dust, and steel girders, abandoned and desolate. Here and there the lower part of the church walls still stand as a reminder. It is a memorial to man's stand for I.F.G. (Independence From God.) Daylight is fading from the late afternoon sky, the lights are appearing in cosy looking houses on the other side of the street. In the gardens opposite the church the trees are nearly bare now and stand silhouetted against the wintry sunset. The few remaining brittle brown leaves rustle softly in the merest breeze and flutter dryly to join the carpet of dead leaves that already covers the grass below. A few crows caw raucously, and the pigeons that once roosted in the church, having found new accommodation on the ledge of the adjoining property, return to the ledge and mutter sleepily to one another, a cooing and gurgling sound that is simultaneously gentle but guttural.

Four figures stand in the shadows on the corner of the site. They were there at the beginning, but nobody noticed them then, although some people heard their voices. The oldest of the four women is the one people notice the least. She has a sweet face, but with her faded light brown hair turning grey and her plump, homely figure dressed in comfortable, practical clothing rather than the latest fashions, people tend to by-pass her in favour of her more exciting cousins. If they only took time to notice, they would see that her grey-blue eyes hold a depth of suffering and compassion, and a compelling honesty that speaks of a friend who would never let you down. The three cousins are a much more eye-catching proposition. They are not unalike, each dressed in colourful up-to-the-minute fashions, adorned with bright costume jewellery, with their hair tinted and elegantly coiffed, their skins tanned and glowing from a recent Mediterranean holiday, and their make-up perfect. The names of the three sisters are Rumour, Gossip and Greed -- their surname, of course, being Jones -- and their unobtrusive cousin is called Mercy.

Rumour, Gossip and Greed are holding an animated conversation about how Greed seduced a local businessman, and Rumour, who has a rather carrying voice, is telling of unpaid bills and broken contracts. Gossip can't wait to go and tell her neighbour who doesn't like the gentleman in question anyway. Meanwhile Mercy says quietly that, if you can't say something nice about someone, you shouldn't say anything at all, but no one pays any attention to her.

Again the curious fact is obvious: now that the church building has been reduced from the neglected, shabby and forlorn red sandstone building that it was to a neglected, shabby and forlorn heap of rubble, the fading light of the wintry sun reaches into corners that it never reached before. Be careful, however, before you jump to conclusions, because another of Moloch Jones' names is Lucifer.

I would point out, for those who have never studied Latin, that Lucifer means "bearer of light." He is also known to be the father of lies, the thief who comes only to steal and kill and destroy.

With love from Karen

Part Four

Weighty Matters

The Sugar-Dragon

THE SUGAR-DRAGON lurks
Within my kitchen;
He's hiding there
Behind the fridge,
Just waiting
To pounce on me
In an unguarded moment.

He waits in other places too -
In my friends' houses
Behind whichever chair I choose.
In his presence
My will-power crumbles;
Quivering with indecision,
He slinks away defeated,
Telling me
He'll be stronger ..
Tomorrow.

The sugar-dragon
Is such a pretty thing.
His sparkling scales
Are sugar-frosted;
His eyes are liquid fire
Of crimson cherry brandy.
His nostrils flare, but
No fearful hellish stench he breathes
No, no! Rather, the sweet perfume
Of new baked bread, (to go with jam),
Or cookies warm,
Or fruit cake lush
All covered thick with marzipan;
Or doughnuts dripping fudge!

No claws will tear my flesh, no, no!

But, rather, softest hands he has
Bearing plates of goodies sweet:
Chocolate-coated langues-de-chat,
Shortbread made with butter,
Christmas pud and mince-pies too,
And trifle thick with cream.

The sugar-dragon
Whispers
Seductive words of comfort,
And steals all common-sense.

My friends succumb
To his enchantment too.
"Just one little slice," they say,
"Won't do you any harm. I baked it
Specially for you!"
And just to please,
I find
My hand is reaching out,
All by itself, to take just one.
He leads us all,
My friends and me,
Into his Sugar Fairyland!

But once we're there
The sweetness changes
Most horrendously.
His soft white hands
Transform
Into talons sharp
That tear your flesh with cravings:
A desire for more
That can never
Be appeased.

His companions
Sidle in beside him,
Greedy for my body.
Obesity and Stroke,
Diabetes,
Cancer and Tooth Decay.
Atherosclerosis,
Arthritis,
Coronary and more.
They all queue up
To get a share.

And over all presides
The pretty sugar-dragon!

Will no-one set me free
From the monster
That crouches at my door?

Will-power, come back!
I'm ready!
I'll listen to you now.
Come back, come back!
Perhaps all is not lost.
I'll try again.
Tomorrow.

For all the Sugar dragon's victims,
with love from Karen

Doom of the Sugar-Dragon

YESTERDAY
Tomorrow
Became
Today!
I tried and tried and tried!
When he wasn't looking
I shoved him in the cupboard,
That sugar-dragon sweet!
I pushed him in
And slammed the door
With all my might,
And then I leaned on it
As hard as hard could be.
He screamed
And shouted,
Yelled and bawled,
But I would not give in!! No way!

For hours and hours
We battled,
He and I, and I, of course,
Had Will-Power on my side.

Dear old Will!
He's somewhat bruised and
Rather battle-weary.
All day long we
Were on the winning side.
But suddenly
Will and I got tired.

One little moment,
That was all,

A flicker of indecision!
The sugar-dragon gained
Advantage,
And sneaked his fingers through
The merest chink
In that old cupboard door.
Just one spoon of sugar was his weapon -
That was all!!
He slipped it down my unresisting throat,
And I was lost.
Two biscuits followed,
Then bread and jam,
And last of all, a chunk of cheese!!

But that all happened on the tomorrow
That was today
Yesterday, and yesterday
Today was still tomorrow,
And now tomorrow is still ahead!!
As long as there is still
Tomorrow
Then there's always Hope!!

I'll go and speak
To my friend Will
And do my best
To strengthen him today
For tomorrow!
We'll shut that sugar-dragon in
And barricade the door.

And anyway,
We've got friends
In High Places!
We've got Truth,
And Courage,
Patience, Peace
And Joy,

To name just some.
And there's more!
There's Gentleness
And Love,
Faithfulness and Kindness too,
Goodness and Self-control!
The promises of God above
Are all available
For me!!
And they spell doom
For that old sugar-dragon.

The battle is already won,
But sometimes
A skirmish must be fought.

It's up to me -
I must remember
To wear the armour
Of my God,
And He'll not let me down.

With love from Karen

Weight loss now, ask me how

Another day,
Another diet!
It's new, improved!
I gotta try it!

The very first one
My doctor did set
Was so full of don'ts
That I mustn't forget.

Thou shalt not eat
Any food that's sweet!
And certainly not
That soup in the pot!
No sausages, pies
Or tasty French fries,
No puddings or cakes
Or Cadbury's flakes.

And no ice-cream!!
My childhood dream!
No ice-cream?
No, none.

Okay, I'm done.
That diet's gone
For a Burton.

The next delight
To meet my sight
Was a powder pink
That would make me shrink!!
It didn't.

And then there came the calorie!
Life would be simple now.

All you did was take a vow
To count a thousand,
Not one more,
And if you really wanted
You could score
A mere
Eight hundred of the little mites
That would use
About five bites
Of my mum's fruit cake!!

So half a lettuce leaf you ate,
Chopped fine
And spread around the plate
It looked
Quite tantalizing!!

Another day, another diet!
I've tried the lot,
I thought!
But no, another bright idea
Has hit the scene.
We'll try psychology …
You gotta keep your mind
Occupied
With other things!
"Mummy, what's for tea!!"
"Karen, do have
another piece of cake!
It's really quite okay,
It's baked with Flora …
Very healthy!!"

So back to counting calories.
That cake was
783
and a ½
which leaves

416
and a ½ to do
from now till midnight!
No, you say, that sum's not right!
But yes, it is!! You see,
They changed the rules
In '73
And said
That more was better.
So now I can have just one Creme egg
With my dainty chopped up
Lettuce leaves!!
And better still,
That leaves enough
To have a cup of tea.
With milk!!

But look, hey, hey
A bright new thing
All the way
From the U.S.A.
Called 'erbalife
It'll end the strife
In my life!!

3,2,1
it's easy done!
Three times the tablets every day
And then two shakes
Is all it takes
With one main meal
To complete the deal!
This IS easy,
I did think,
And quite fantastic!
Boy, did I shrink!!

Skinny me was something new
And for a while I was not blue!
But then things changed
And so did I.
Square one
Was where I landed back.

So then along came
Atkins!
A bucket of cream
Was such a dream
And cheese galore
Who could ask for more!
I stuffed and stuffed
And didn't get fatter!
I didn't get thinner
But that didn't matter
'cos I could eat cream
and pounds of butter!
Yum, yum!

Then came the day
When I just couldn't face
The bacon and eggs
That sat in my place
For breakfast.

I dithered
And swithered.
What should I do?
My friends all said
You're fine as you are!
It became easier now
To take the car,
Not walk.
You're a granny now
The friends all said,
And you look fine

As you are.

But my kids said something else!
So just for them
I started again.
Another day, another diet.
Here's something new,
You gotta try it.

Potatoes were out,
And now they're' in.
Pasta's great
And I'm getting thin!
Butter's out
Without a doubt.
I found another diet
So I just had to try it!!!

With love from Karen

Part Five

Spiders, Dentists, etc

Ode to my Favourite Dentist

I climbed the stairs
With many prayers.
Twenty-three
There be,
That's stairs
Not prayers.
There's far more prayers
Than stairs!

It's then
That I wonder
What word rhymest
With dentist.
He suggested pessimist,
I hoped optimist.

A word that rhymes with molar
Is Zola
(As in Budd.)

She runs.
Maybe I should too.
Hypodemic nerdle
Rhymes with hurdle.
I'd rather jump a hurdle
Than face the dentist's nerdle.

But if I jump or run
It's not much fun --
The tooth comes too!
So the thing to do
Is go.
Oh woe!

So I climb the stairs
Twenty-three in all
To seek the help
Of my friend Paul.

There's a hole in my molar
Dear Paul, dear Paul,
There's a hole in my molar,
So what can you do?

I'll drill it and fill it,
Said Paul, said Paul,
I'll drill it and fill it.
This won't hurt at all!!

So first Paul did the drillin'
And next put in the fillin'
Then he sends the bill in!
This won't hurt at all!!

Dedicated to our favourite dentist
With love from Karen

A Better Ode To My Favourite Dentist

In days of yore
When a tooth got sore
You'd have to get drunk
As a partying skunk
Before you went
In a whisky-filled mist
To your dent-
ist.

He'd sit you down there
In his dreaded chair.
He'd tug and he'd heave
And then you'd leave.
He was ruthless!!
And you were toothless!

But now things have changed
With the recent appliance
Of technical science.
Finely-honed skill
Means the man with the drill
Can soothe all your fears
And banish the tears,
But better still –
You leave the chair
With your teeth still there!
(Well, mostly,
Even though costly!)

Without you, Paul,
To fix my teeth
My life would all
Be full of grief.

My smile would go
And my woe would show!
I'd look like a freak!
I'd be up the creek!

So I thank you now
For your care and attention.
That hole in my purse
I won't even mention!
You're worth every penny!
Though I had to lose one,
I've still got many!
And I hope they last
As long as me
'Cos I plan to live
To a hundred and three.
(At least!)

And if I said
That I don't dread
The day you retire
I'd be a liar.
If ever I find
Some brilliant mind
That can clone you,
I'll phone you!
So please don't go
For a very long time –
Your dentistry skills
Are quite sublime!

With love from Karen

The spider

For Steven

Write, my friend said. Write what, I said. Write about anything, he said, take a year in your life and write about that, he said. O.K., I said, and immediately started to feel happier because it's what I really wanted to do all along but didn't know it, especially after I encountered that magical gadget, the word-preciser, which allows me to write precisely what I want to say, and to express all my complicated feelings in a way which helps me to come to terms with life.

O.K. I will write about spiders, one in particular. I was sitting in the bathroom, wrapped in my bath towel, contemplating (as I always do in the bathroom) the deeper things in life, like sandwich fillings, when all of a sudden I noticed this spider clinging to the shower curtain, absolutely motionless. I remained motionless too, thinking that I ought to remove it because its presence would upset Catriona more than just a little.

It's funny how spiders like certain houses. Ours, for instance. Our house will never be a "designer pad". It's not typical of a Bearsden residence -- in fact it's not typical of any residence I've ever come across before, and while certain members of my wider family shake their heads despairingly, the strange thing is that our kids wouldn't have us live anywhere else.

To reach us, for a start, you have to negotiate the mess that the plumbers left when they eventually came to take away the lead pipes by digging up all the concrete at the gate. If you arrive before the rain, you're O.K. - you can get through the hedge, past the thistles and foxgloves, past the designer heap of rubble too. That was left by the other guys when they removed the dry-rot, rising damp and various other anti-social graces which adorned our bathroom in the days of the lead pipes. After all these adventures you have reached the bottom of the steps, whereafter you encounter the fuchsia (entwined with the rambling pink roses) which from time to time meets with the forsythia on the other side, and creates the perfect setting for Prince Charming to come and rescue the Sleeping Beauty. As I said, if you arrive before the rain does, you're O.K., assuming you didn't mind your clothes being snagged by the wayward rambling rose. If the rain got there first, you would have been advised to wear oilskins and welly boots for this part of your visit. Strangely enough, spiders are not daunted by the prospect of this entry into our house. In fact they positively love it, arriving in hordes without welly boots, and nine times out of ten go straight to Catriona's bedroom where they lurk smugly, waiting for her to find them on the ceiling at 4.00 a.m. (Who else do you know who actually looks at their ceiling if they happen to waken at 4.00 a.m.?)

The remaining one out of ten makes a bee-line (I would actually have thought spider-line was a much more appropriate phrase) for the bathroom, where as often as not it is Catriona who finds It, and as often as not it is I who carefully remove it to the top of the steps and lay it gently beside the forsythia (which sometimes meets with the fuchsia thereby creating a bridge for spiders to cross to the other side!!)

By some remarkable instinct these delightful and determined little creatures go straight back to the exact place from which I just ever so carefully removed them.

It is, of course, a little known fact that all spiders are called Betty. The reliable source of this riveting piece of information is my mother-in-law who has a sister called Betty. She also has a sister called Dallas after whom a cow was named. I don't know why.

Having filled you in on how the spider came to be in my bathroom, I will get back to where I was. The spider clung to the shower curtain without flinching, and I contemplated it without flinching, and I wondered what it was thinking about while I was thinking about it. Probably nothing at all. I don't think I am capable of thinking about nothing at all -- I might *say* I was thinking about nothing at all, but that would be a lie, and in spite of my claims to be a very honest lady, there are times when I would rather that people did not know what was going on in my mind. However, I rather think that the spider is not equipped with my complicated emotions and any motives it may have (for instance food or reproduction) are more likely to be purely instinctive. Its compulsive urge to get right back to where it was removed from must be some kind of automatic pilot. This is all because it is not made in the image of God, Who says that He made us humans in His image. If He is a Creator as He says He is, then if we are made in His image we must be creative too or else we are miserable. If we are not being creative, then either we are being spiders or we are being destructive, which is in its own way creative - as in creating merry hell, which a lot of people do when they don't have a right direction to follow. Destruction need not necessarily be negative. Take for instance what the demolition company is doing with the former factory down the road from us. The demolition of something that is no longer useful, and the making tidy of a space that will be used to build something functional (and hopefully pleasing to the eye) is positively creative.

So it is with us human beings. Sometimes God has to demolish old attitudes and motives which served a purpose at a given time, and then he builds something new in the old space. As He chips away at the old concrete it can be sore, and sometimes it is a slow process with many weeks passing and no obvious activity, but always in the background the master architect has a plan.

Ah well, so much for spiders and demolition men. Life goes on, dishes must be washed. What's it all about anyway?

With love from Karen

It is now almost a year since my friend Steven said write, and I said write what, and he said write about anything.

Once again it is a Sunday morning, and I am sitting in the bath. What a delicious sensation it is, to step into the green-blue warmth of the silky waters and lower weary, painful joints and aching muscles into the soothing depths, and to let the heat wash away the day's stresses and strains while the gentle lapping and splashing of the water lulls the tight brain to sleep.

But not completely to sleep. Thoughts start to drift through my semiconsciousness, and gradually take form. Ideas that have been pushed out of the way in the hustle and bustle of a week's business start to surface and demand attention. This is the time when the deeper philosophies of life are formulated, and although I don't make it to church for my spiritual nourishment, I like to think that God gets my attention for a while.

For instance, the thought occurred to me that going to church is a bit like putting Domestos down the loo. If one neglects to do this task, one has noticed that both visibly and atmospherically the quality of life is diminished. There is a build-up of gunge (for want of a less polite description), and this begins to be offensive to say the least, not just to the eye, but also to the nose, and probably to the health of one and all too. Therefore, one pours a hefty dose of Domestos down the loo, and hey, presto, zoom!!! - after about half an hour, all is clean and sweet-smelling and healthy again. With an encouraging result like this, one might even be so excited that one rushes off and gets rubber gloves and cloths and such-like exciting things and cleans the rest of the bathroom.

On the other hand, one might not bother with the rushing bit. One might just sit on the edge of the bath (having got out of it first) and set to developing more of life's deeper philosophies, like the slater.

Slater?, I hear you ask. What slater? Are you referring to the man who mends the roof? No, I don't think so, I reply, now becoming a bit uncertain myself and resolving to go and look up the dictionary for the word "slater". We always called them slaters when I was young, and somewhere I think I read something about them being the remnants of a prehistoric type of creature. Anyway, there is one of these strange little creatures creeping up the shower curtain, in almost the same place as the spider which rocketed me to international literary acclaim last year. (Well, by 'international' I mean that my fans include my husband who was born in Japan, my sister in Dollar and my auntie who lived in America for a while!)

Life continues to be full of wonder at the beings who share my bathroom with me. Slaters, spiders and now, this very morning, the largest bumble bee you ever saw, who, without a by-your-leave or a please, not even an offer to pay rent, has spent the whole winter sleeping in that hole under the radiator. I guess he thought he owned the place!! Just so long as he (or is it perhaps she, the queen bee?) doesn't expect me to pay rent! How many more of the good Lord's little creatures are snuggling in around the place, I ask myself. I do hope there's no wasps. If ever you can explain to me what the purpose of wasps is, I'd be grateful for the information! Ah well, enough of this burble. There's things to do out there ...

Ode to a Spiedme

As I was standing in the shower
For an hour
Getting clean and thinking
While drinking
Tea,

I got a fright.
I didn't scream with all my might!
I stood and shook
Until I took
My mug and caught
In a moment fraught
A large black hairy spiedme.

A spiedme, you say. What's that?
Well, if Muffet
On her tuffet
Ran away
From curds and whey
Because the creature spied her
And sat beside her,
Then this one must be
A spiedme,
Because it did.

I'm glad
I'd finished
The tea.

For Catriona and Charlotte,
with love from Karen

Jenny
(for Janet and Julie, my sandwich makers)

Frail. Fragile. You flittered into my shop the other day, your long legs trailing as you hovered, flitted, darted here and there, seemingly aimlessly, but surely you knew where you were going. Your long thin body suspended mid-air by wings that are transparent, yet veined in such a fine pattern. Your legs are such a piece of engineering. Why so long? Why constructed so? What part do you play in the scheme of things?

Some of us are afraid of you. We do not like you to get caught in our hair, to brush against us, albeit ever so softly, in your innocent flitterings about our space. Environmental Health does not like you - one never knows where you may have trailed those long legs of yours. Do you have feet? We don't know what nasty things you may have walked in or danced over. So you're not welcome in my shop where hygiene is all-important. So now you know, little Jenny, why I went to kill you the other day when you came to visit. But I didn't kill you. It wasn't exactly my fault that you moved just as I did, so that all I got was one of your beautifully constructed, fragile legs. You flitted away, and you left your leg behind. It wasn't the end of the world for you, because you still had quite a lot of legs left - probably five. You creatures never stay still long enough for me to count, and in fact I never thought to count your legs before. It was only when you went away and left one behind that I gave the matter any serious thought at all.

You, little Jenny, were only doing what comes naturally, only doing what you were created for, whatever that may be. I am not a biologist or a naturalist, so I never studied your ways. You were doing what comes naturally to you, and I in turn was reacting aggressively to your presence for two reasons, the first being my human instinct to avoid being tickled by your wings and legs, the fear of you being caught in my hair, and the second being because the Law requires me to exterminate beasties that might contaminate the food I prepare for other people.

What I wonder is this: was it this way with Mr. Hitler and his friends? Surely they were reacting aggressively to that which made them afraid, a massive sense of insecurity because no-one had taught them about loving and understanding their fellow beings, because they followed a Law which required them to kill, and hurt, and subjugate everything and everyone which stood in their way. In their own way, they were doing right because they were earnestly obeying the law which they had learned to follow.

Basically there are two forces in our world. The good and the bad. The light and the dark. There is a God of the good and the light, and there is a god of the bad and the dark.

The law of the first is love, which says that it is patient, and kind; that it does not envy, it does not boast, it is not proud; neither is it rude, nor self-seeking, nor is it easily angered; it does not keep a record of wrongs; it does not delight in evil but it does rejoice with the truth; it always protects, always trusts, always hopes, always perseveres, and never fails. This is a love which respects the other person and says that I should love my neighbour as I love myself. (Interesting question: how much does one respect oneself? And if one does not respect oneself, then how much can one respect another person?)

And then there is the law of the bad and the dark god. This god has the name Lucifer, which is translated from the Latin and means "bearer of light". He is also referred to as "the father of lies", and if you put two and two together, the obvious inference is that he wants you to think that he is the bearer of light when all along he does anything but bring light into the situation. This god wishes only to deceive, to steal and to destroy. The problem, of course, is to know when which God is doing what, and if you're not being awfully concerned with either God, then how 'on earth' are you to know?

A major problem is that without some assistance from the God of the good and the light (assistance which apparently we have to seek actively), then it is very difficult to love with patience, kindness, unselfishness and all that, because mostly we do what comes naturally, like you, dear Jenny

Long-Legs, and trail our long legs (with feet attached) through all the muck and pigeon droppings which abound in this life and inadvertently spread impatience, unkindness, envy, boasting, anger and all that negative stuff.

Take the question of pigeon droppings, for instance. (Well, I know you would rather not, but some of us have no option.) The pigeons are up there, and we are down here, and they doo what they doo (if you'll forgive the pun) and we have to walk on the pavement to get from there to here and back again. What was God actually planning when he invented pigeons? Would it not have been possible for him to have invented pretty birds with no by-products?

And whatever was He thinking of when He thought up the stripey stinging buzziness of a wasp? A beautiful soft furry bee I can understand, because from bees come honey which goes superbly with toast and butter. (Unfortunately buttered toast and honey makes you fat, so maybe this wasn't such a bright invention after all.)

However, to get back to the common wasp - one does have to wonder if the Almighty Eternal Plan couldn't have gone ahead without wasps, not to mention spiders. I did already mention spiders in an earlier treatise, but perhaps, dear Jenny, you haven't read that yet, and probably Jenny Long-Legses don't go in for much reading, so I will take the liberty of saying that my daughter Catriona would be very happy if Our Great Big Wonderful God could let spiders become extinct right now, if not sooner.

Over all the generations since time began, Jenny, we mortals have questioned Our God about His purposes, because we have limited vision down here and can only truly understand what is within our own experience, and by nature, we do not wish to understand unless we have seen it, felt it, touched it, smelt it, heard it, tasted it, liked it, disliked it, loved it, hated it, been frightened by it or been comforted by it for our very own selves. And once again, Jenny, like Job in the Bible, I am doing just that thing: I am full of questions for the God of the good and the light about the bad and the dark, and sometimes I even reach that point in my questioning when I can say not so much "why?" as "what?" - "Why did You do that, God?" is replaced by "What are You trying to teach me through this experience?"

Well, little Jenny, as I write this to you, you are now lying dead on a piece of kitchen paper, slaughtered by my hand as you struggled to continue your frail existence with one leg less than you should have had.

It was not a mindless human act.   As I already said, the Law required it.
Nor was it done without thought for my victim.   The thought that prevails
is weary sadness that the world is groaning under a near intolerable weight
of violence and cruelty and selfishness, and that if we did not have a God
of Hope, then the struggle would be worthless.   Dear Jenny, forgive me.

With love from Karen

Written during the time
when we had 'Munchies'
the sandwich business, and
we were working 90 hours a week.

Part Six

Words of Wisdom for my Family

The Graduation
For Catriona

*In 1993 we had the privilege of launching another daughter
out into the big wide world with academic qualifications, and
this is the 'word-picture' of that lovely event.*

Write, said my friend, and I answered write what. Write about a
year in your life, he said, so I said O.K. and definitely feel happier writing
things down.

Creative it is, this writing, and being made in the Image of God
Himself, I am doing what He made me for.

What's it all about, I asked, and I think the answer must be that it's all
about glorifying God by doing whatever creative thing He made us for.

Graduating, for instance. I didn't myself, but yesterday my child did,
and to see her standing there in her black gown and beautiful fur-edged
green hood, looking so beautiful herself, so academically distinguished,
was one of life's fulfilling moments.

On Thursday night, in Glasgow, it poured with rain. Early on Friday
we left the grey skies clearing nicely, and drove eastward to Dundee. On
the high ground at Auchterarder the skies lowered to meet the moors,
and cars emerged from the murkiness with their headlights on, but in our
optimism we kept hoping that the sun would shine on Dundee. After
all, did the sun not shine on previous graduations at Heriot-Watt in
Edinburgh for our older two? Could the Good Lord not arrange the same
for our third? Heavy drops of rain fell as we neared Dundee itself, but
stopped, and we went on hoping.

The large straw hat with enormous cerise flower bore the Instructions
"Do not wear in the rain", so we had brought an even more enormous
stripey umbrella (free with somebody's wine.) Just In case. The enormous
hat was being worn because Judith's Mum was wearing one because I was
wearing one. The hat was The Thing, although the new blue silk dress was
fun to buy as well (along with three days total starvation so that the waist
would fit properly.) The high-heeled shoes were the true martyrdom for
the occasion, and as we left the car parked at the railway station, and Ian
strode ahead in kilt with umbrella (just in case!), I teetered along behind
doing an admirable imitation of an elegant lady. (I swear nobody would
know at that point what an imposter I was being!)

We reached the Caird Hall to find the square thronged with people, graduands resplendent in their best suits, kilts and dresses, proudly wearing their black gowns and forty-shades-of-green hoods (there were some other colours too, gold, white and blue) - and parents of all shapes and sizes in varying degrees of fashion. Quite a lot of hats, but naturally none as good as mine!!

Cameras were clicking like mad, and there was an air of excitement as the appointed hour for the Graduation drew near. We all made our way up the imposing steps to the entrance, and all of a sudden, there was *our* special graduand, looking absolutely radiant, auburn hair tied back loosely, eyes very blue, wearing her great-grandmother's beautiful moonstone pendant and her pretty new dress, but most impressive of all, the black gown and the hood, a soft bluey green, edged with white fur.

We found seats In the gallery where we could see all the proceedings and Catriona too, and waited for It all to begin. There was a flurry of panic as Catriona appeared briefly, to find something in her handbag which I was looking after, and then she disappeared again threatening to shoot the organist who was keeping us entertained, but obviously not doing the same for her.

The strains of *Gaudeamus Igitur* filled the hall, which was now filled to capacity. Memories of my own days at St. Andrews flooded back, making me think how futile it was to get so intensely screwed-up about life, when, looking back now, I can see that God had something better up His sleeve for me, if I had only known then to trust Him as I (try to) do now. The platform party, colourful and sedate, wended their way down the hall and onto the platform where they complemented the tubs of flowers arranged on the tiers behind them.

There was an admirably brief introductory speech by the Principal of Duncan of Jordanstone College of Art, who is about to retire, and then the real business of conferring degrees began. One by one the plain pine green hoods filed up, the name was read out, the head was zapped (none too gently, we later learned) with the traditional Dundee Bonnet (specially created for these occasions) and the newly graduated student left the stage - some walked sedately, some turned and waved to their admiring fans. All were clapped, occasionally more enthusiastically, as with the almost-blind graduate. The pine greens were followed by the other shades of green, the golds, the whites, the blue architects, and then, near the end came our bluey green Town And Regional Planners. At one point the

Dundee Bunnet was dropped on its way to the graduand's head, and there was a momentary pause because presumably neither Principal nor graduand knew which of them should pick it up. The clapping becomes tiring on the wrists, but fortunately not all the clappers stop for a rest at the same time, so it is a continuous sound. As my Dad always used to observe, it sounds like a running bath. I found myself sitting more upright, hand poised on camera, as Catriona's turn approached, and as always on these momentous occasions, I viewed the Actual Moment of Graduation through the viewfinder of my little camera.

Afterwards she asked if I had seen her looking up at us! ? Sadly not, as my eyesight through the viewfinder is a bit limited.

Not long to go, we thought as we gasped for a cup of coffee, but still there were the four honorary degrees to be conferred, with a potted life history of each to be given first. Then it was all over, and the platform party wended out again, and we all followed.

Now came the task of finding our new graduate, and the bright idea of meeting in the square outside had lost some of its appeal since the rain which had been washing the streets of Glasgow the previous night was now doing the same to Dundee, with a vengeance!! On the imposing Caird Hall steps the throngs were milling again, groups of classes trying to get together for photographs, other individuals looking for parents, taking photos of each other with parents, lots of umbrellas bobbing about and all the forty-shades-of-green hoods turning to other shades of green as they got wetter by the second. After minimal photography we decided to bolt for the Rep Theatre Bar to have a drink before going on to our lunchtime rendezvous with Rachel and family at a Chinese Restaurant.

Ian bravely held the large umbrella over The Hat and The Graduate as we sploshed through the streets to our destinations, and eventually eleven of us sat down to the relaxed atmosphere of the Chinese Restaurant and sampled a variety of known and unknown dishes. A happy time was had as the various parents got to know each other better and the new graduates unwound a little from the tension of the morning.

Two hours later we emerged to find that the rain had stopped and we could proceed with umbrella furled to The Garden Party. Catriona and Rachel (with Rachel's boyfriend Alec) disappeared off to have The Photographs taken (the ones that proud parents and grandparents display in posh frames to impress the next generation), and Ian and I wandered off to explore the University while waiting to be ferried by bus to the

Botanic Gardens for the Garden Party. My feet were beginning to object to prolonged elegance, but I soldiered on womanfully as befits the mother of a graduate.

We never knew before that there was a Botanic Garden in Dundee, but, sure enough, at the far west end of the city, amongst the big houses and overlooking the Tay, we found ourselves walking on paths (awash with mud) amidst rain sodden lawns, surrounded by beautiful trees and shrubs, a greenhouse here and a pond there, and eventually a marquee, and of course, lots of people.

In the marquee there were tables with glasses of wine (and orange for me), and waitresses running around with inexhaustible supplies of strawberry tarts, and sandwiches too. We ventured out, but didn't stay out long because the rain started again. The unmistakable smell of grass-in-tent filled the marquee, and as it filled up with more and more people it began to get stuffy and breathless. We chatted with Rachel's Mum and her husband for a while, all the time watching for Catriona and Rachel to arrive. Eventually Ian went off to look and discovered that they had been watching for us in the other marquee and, like ourselves, had not realised that there were two marquees!

The rain had stopped again, and we spent a while bravely battling our way back and forth through the madding, milling, thronging, happy crowds (ankle deep in mud) while Catriona tried to catch up with Maddy (whom we did find, along with Father and wife and baby sister and Mother and husband) and Judith (whom she never did find, although we had seen her).

We eventually stopped thronging back and forth, which was just as well because my feet were totally overcome by elegance, and I was by now standing from time to time, when no one was looking, in my stocking soles on the soggy grass. (Bliss. Total destruction of carefully cultivated image of an elegant lady.) For a while we just stood there amidst all these beautiful trees and shrubs, which were by now adorned around their bases with clumps of empty wine glasses, and we chatted with Rachel's Dad and Rachel and Alec, and sometimes Tracy and Rhonda would join in, and more photos were taken.

And then it was time to go.

We hopped back on a bus that was taking the madding-milling crowds back to the University, and the Good Lord in his kindness arranged that the bus would go right past the railway station and allow my feet to get to the car without further agony. And so we left Dundee, and drove westwards, not so much into the setting sun, but toward hills swathed in misty grey clouds, leaving behind us our happy graduate, still looking beautiful and about to enjoy her last night of Dundee student revelry before rounding the whole thing off the following night with the Graduation Ball at Glasgow's illustrious Hilton Hotel. Thank you, God, for another child launched into the world with academic qualifications.

With love from Karen

The greatest command

In my life, two sayings have had huge significance for me.

The first was something my mother said in her later years, when she was ill with cancer. She said to my sister-in-law that she had learned to like herself better once she stopped being so critical of other people.

The second was what my younger sister said to me when I was going through a particularly bad spell of depression. She said, "God does not ask you to account for the talents he didn't give you. He only asks you to account for the talents he did give you."

You may not think those two comments are related at all, but the other day I realised just how very basic to health and happiness these two concepts are.

I was lying in the bath contemplating, as I always do in the bath. I was contemplating the fact that I am surrounded by crumbling relationships and heart-broken or dissatisfied people. It seems that society is being engulfed by unhappiness and dissatisfaction.

I suddenly realised that a common factor in so many cases is that people seem to be constantly judging and criticising others, looking for the worst in others in order to build their own self-esteem, to give themselves value in a chaotic society, where worth is as elusive as looking for a shape-shifter (those who watch Deep Space Nine will know to what I refer.)

So many of us have insecurities and hang-ups, because of the false values promoted by our godless society, that it is now a chronic disease of epidemic proportions. If only we could see ourselves as individuals created by God, each one unique, and each one of inestimable value to the God who created us in his own image.

As my mother discovered, when she stopped criticizing others, she learned to like herself better. What a gift to have received before it was too late.

I have seen two youngsters whose minds have been damaged by a mother who constantly decried the other members of the family, telling them how awful their relations are. One of the two has just broken free and is rejoicing in finding out for herself how nice her awful relations really are.

I have seen husbands and wives, or as the modern way is, "partners", tear each other apart by constant criticism and judgemental attitude. How I wish that those basics tenets of the Bible could be dinned into the human race at birth, and how much easier our lives would be.

It seems however that the Good Lord has given us the task of using our own wits and common sense to find the path through the wondrous landscape of life, filled as it is with deserts, jungles, mountains, stony ground and wide fertile plains filled with beauty. Like The Pilgrim's Progress, The Lord of The Rings, and The Lion, The Witch and The Wardrobe, life is truly a journey.

The tragedy of modern life is that we threw away the guidebook, and we thought that Science was the answer to making all paths smooth and painless.

It occurs to me that the Good Lord has given us this task because He knows that, if we are created in His image, then we will prove it by finding the path, and then we will indeed be fit to join him in that place of ultimate perfection called Eternity.

However, in the meantime, we have thrown away the guidebook and are struggling to find the way using this thing we call Self.

I don't really like the expression "self-esteem", as it promotes the idea that "self" is at the centre of the Universe, not God. And all that "self" has done for me is to get me into trouble. Whoever said that sin is a three letter word with "I" in the middle had it well sussed-out. Those who promote "self" have not realised that there is an immutable law which says that mankind must answer to some kind of higher authority, and if mankind is not answering to God then he is answering to the Devil. The tragedy is that the Devil is a sneaky bastard who keeps his evil intentions up his sleeve and lets the godless man think that he himself is in control. Is he tookey!!!

A better word for "self-esteem" might be "Godworth". And I would suggest that there is no such thing as "low Godworth". It just couldn't exist!! In God's eyes, we are his children, each one unique, special, infinitely loved and cherished. I nearly cry when I think how much I love my own children, and how much I would do to protect them, to heal them, to nourish them, to comfort them, to secure their happiness, contentment, peace and complete fulfilment. What is the sum of these words "protect, heal, nourish, comfort, make happy, content, peaceful and fulfilled"? I would suggest that the sum is to love and cherish.

If I am loved and cherished, then my natural instinct will be to love and cherish in return, and to trust. But if that is missing, then what? The path through life in this ungodworthy state must be truly rough and filled with anguish and grief.

Just suppose for a minute that you found the guidebook, and discovered that the right path was the one where you looked for the best in each person you encountered. You would greet them with a smile instead of a cold shoulder. And they would smile at you, and at once your day would brighten. If instead of saying to someone that their work is not really very good and watching them slink away in dejection, suppose you told them that they had made a really good effort and you appreciated the time they had spent labouring on the project, think of the glow of warm feeling that person would have. The glow would rebound and warm you both. Suppose that you imagined yourself in the hurting person's shoes, how would you behave in their circumstances? Be honest now.

Now, to get back to the question of accounting to God for the talents he gave you. Perhaps you are deeply distressed at the fact that you simply cannot manage to work a computer, and that you feel such an idiot because all your friends can. When computers are mentioned you just go into your shell and wish you could be somewhere else. I'm like that with housework, and I go into the house of my beloved aunt, and her house is like something out of "Homes and Gardens" magazine, and my house is like something out of "Refuse Collectors' Magazine" or "Bins and Tips of The World". I feel so helpless and inadequate because, try as I will, I cannot compete with her ruthless tidiness and uncluttered serenity. We are so different!!

If I allow myself to dwell on this inadequacy, I become more and more dissatisfied and unhappy, and my mood becomes irritable and I become sorry for myself (that word "self" again!!), and think about how unfair it is that I have to live as I do. I'm not even going to put into print the unpleasant path that my thoughts wander down.

However, if I think of the talents that God gave me, I suddenly find pleasure in all sorts of things, and I'm ready to face the world with a smile. I feel fulfilled by the things I can do, and my godworthiness surfaces in good shape. Then I begin to like myself.

This is where my mother's discovery and my sister's words are in line with each other.

This is where you discover that looking for the best in other people and liking yourself actually come together to fulfil what Jesus said was the greatest command of the ten commandments.

"Love one another as I have loved you."

I can't help but feel that if you start looking for the best in other people, you will find your own true godworthiness and the world will become that little bit happier for everyone.

With love from Karen

No God
(for some of my nearest and dearest)

There is no God, you say.
You look at life
A different way
From me.
So there are questions
I must ask. Like,
How did all things come to be?

And when you get that feeling,
(I'm sure you've felt it too),
That overwhelming ache of joy
From deep within your heart,
When sunset enflames the wide blue sky
Sending golden rays across the sea,
Or larksong's purity thrills the air,
Or a baby laughs in innocent glee,
Who do you thank?
If not God,
Then who?
Or what?

So tell me, please.
I need to know.

A Big Bang started off the lot,
Say some.
But who, I ask,
Made this Big Bang?

And out there I see stars,
And planets spinning all around
Our earth.
Does some strange force
Control their course,
Or do they move at random?

And beyond those stars comes what?
Well, you say,
There's more,
And more of much the same.
It's called 'Infinity'.
So what, I ask, goes on
Beyond 'Infinity'?

The whole idea's too big
For me.
I find it
Quite unnerving.
My comfort comes
From knowing God,
And knowing
That he knows the things
That are too big for me.

But maybe you
Find it all quite simple
To have no God?
Maybe you
Prefer to be in charge
Of everything
Yourself?
No Higher Power
To answer to.
That's fine.

But if things go wrong
As they sometimes do
For me and you,
How do you cope?
Tell me, please,
I want to know.
I'm concerned for you
That there's some pain there
That you can't resolve

And have no comfort,
No God to touch the hurt
And take away the tears.

I love the God
Who made the trees
And all the gifts that cheer me:
Simple things,
Like the cat that purrs,
And the dog that barks and wags her tail,
The gleaming brambles on our walk
And the gentle mist that swathes the hill.
Colours rich and changing seasons,
My whole life overflows with reasons
To love this God who gives so much.

But most of all He fills my life
With people whom I love,
And they love me.
And by that love I measure
The inestimable treasure
Of His love for me.
But back to base.
There is no God, you say.

And I ask once more,
Who do you thank?
And how do you cope?
And anyway
What's out there
Beyond 'Infinity'?

Could it be,
I ask myself,
That your soul still sleeps
And needs
To be awakened?

It's the only thing
That I can think
Is the answer to my question.

I wonder how,
If I were God,
And I had created Creation,
How (on earth) would I get
The attention of those
Who deny
My very existence?

The lonely Jew
On his terrible tree
Was the man God chose
For humanity.
He showed the way
At Calvary,
Though Heaven knows
What God had to pay.

If I am wrong
And there is no God,
Then all that I lose is a myth,
Pie in the sky
When I die by and by.
But if you are wrong
And there is a God
And Heaven and angels and Hell,
Not to mention
Damnation,
Then for Heaven's sake
What will it take
For the God of Creation
To grab your attention?
And I wonder still
Who God will use
Or what He will do

To let you know
That He cares for you.

But I know I'm not wrong
For I've felt, very near,
His presence so real
In a time of great fear.
At a time when I walked
In a highland glen
And the shadow of death
Hovered grimly,
God held me quite safe –
He kept me all night
Until light shone bright
In the morning.
And should things go wrong -
It might happen to you –
I want you to know
That He loves you too
Whatever you do,
And He's only
A prayer away.

So now, my brother, my sister,
My very dear friend,
Of my boring questions this is the end.
I've done my best,
And now the rest
Is up to you – and God.
Go seek, and find
That peace of mind
That only He can grant you.

With love from Karen

Karen's Words for Neil and Charlotte.
6th August, 1994

Val, Neil and Charlotte, Friends and Family,

I know this is a digression from the traditional order of things at weddings, but I could not let you cut into this cake without sharing with you some of the thoughts and the love that went into the making of the cake.

At this point I must tell you that the beautiful design is Charlotte's very own work, and that the execution of the design is the work of our friend and neighbour Mr. David Paton. David has iced wedding cakes for our family for about the last twenty years, although it is only ten years ago that I took on from my mother the role of chief baker of wedding cakes for the family.

Every time I have baked a wedding cake, always from this recipe, I have thought that the ingredient that only I can add is *my* love and prayers for the people concerned. This time I started thinking that the baking of this cake is symbolic of marriage itself – the combining together of a lot of wonderful ingredients, baked long and slow, to produce a rich and satisfying result which is not only enjoyable but nourishes many people.

Let me explain in more detail: take the fruit and spices for instance. Only the very best of ingredients that I could find have gone into this cake. Muscatels are hard to find, and, once found, I hoard them for such occasions as this. First of all, I meticulously remove every stone - a job which takes hours - and then I soak all the fruit in brandy. In marriage too you must remove all the stones lest you choke, or break your teeth, or make yourself sick: the stones are anger, distrust, impatience, criticism, jealousy and suchlike things. Then you must soak your marriage in the spirit of love, which is patience, kindness, forgiveness, humility, good manners, tolerance, unselfishness, honesty, trust, hope and perseverance.

Fruit and spices from many lands represent the international flavour of Neil and Charlotte's marriage: there are influences from Scotland, Portugal, Poland, Japan, Ireland, England, India, Canada and Germany, and possibly more about which I do not know.

In our cake, of course, we have basic ingredients from home too, the butter, eggs and flour are Scottish (I think), and the sugar and treacle are from Safeway!!!! This reflects that in marriage it is not all exotic and romantic, but a lot of pretty basic stuff too, the nitty gritty of daily life, the work, the economising and budgeting, the shopping, cooking, washing, cleaning, ironing, and the D.I.Y. Into this plain and homely mix go the exciting things.

One cannot escape the fruitful connotation of this wedding cake! When the Good Lord told man to go forth and multiply, He was not referring to maths and bank accounts, but rather to the patter of tiny feet. I do have to tell you that, as I spooned the mixture into the smallest tin, I was asking the Good Lord to bless this marriage with children, and that the top tier would all in due time become a christening cake for the first of a new generation of little Macdonalds.

And now one last comment. With the deepest respect for four people in this room, namely Val, Charlotte, Barry and Iris, I would like to tell you why this new daughter-in-law of mine is no ordinary daughter-in-law. Almost exactly six years ago I had a phone-call from Nancy Barreto. She finished by saying, "Thank-you, Karen, for loving Charlotte." I replied, "That's easy! When she's good, she's very, very good, and when she's bad she's horrid, but I love her anyway!" That was the last conversation I had with Nancy before she died one month later, and since then I have regarded loving Charlotte as a special gift left to me by Nancy. Today's celebration is the formalising of a lovely bond that has been in existence for quite a while anyway!

The long, slow baking of this marriage in the warmth of Ian's and my love started way back then, and it looks like being a good, tasty cake!!

Take the knife, my children, and cut the cake with my blessing.

Part Seven

Me and Time

The Perfectionist

Time flies, they told me,
when you
are enjoying yourself.
Ridiculous, I thought.
Why not
time them
when you are bored,
have nothing else to do?

Time them doing what anyway?
Walking on the ceiling?
Treading on my bread and butter,
buzzing menacingly,
threatening
to transfer bacteria
from things
unspeakable
to other things?
(How rude!!)

How long
is the time taken
to do these things?
Would it take me longer?
Answer: Definitely.
(It always does.)

Some people have time.
Time has some people.
She has time.
Time has me.

Work gets done,
in a flash,
perfection missing.

Mission completed anyway,
she goes home.

Me,
I'm stuck
in a time-warp:
my time is not of this planet.
I count bacteria:
the details must be perfect.
In a minute -
or an hour -
or a day -
I will do something.

Which something should I do?
(Have another cup of tea,
while I decide,
and watch
the leaves
opening
on my tree
across the road.)

How long will it take?
I don't know.
Maybe a minute.
Maybe ten,
if something interrupts
and I lose count
of the bacteria
and have to
start again.

On Planet Zog
things are different.
Time does not exist.
So time
can't have people,

which must mean
that all people
have time.
Living on earth
is
difficult
for me:
I time flies.

With love from Karen,
written when we had the sandwich business

The Today Train

It's eight-oh-nine.
One sleepy eye
Focuses
With difficulty.
(The other's in the pillow.)
Inevitably
And inexorably
The Today Train arrives
At Platform One
And I must board right now
- or miss it
And get a later one!

It's empty now,
Apart from sounds
Of pattering rain
And rushing cars.

The Today Train
Pulls away
And slowly
Gathers speed
With my breakfast cup of tea,
Gliding smoothly
On the rails of life's routine.

Who will travel with me,
And what cargo
Will we take?
What stations will we stop at?
At eight-oh-nine, who knows?
Bundles of joy
And loads of care
Must be picked up on the way.
Let's keep the joy

To the journey's end,
But ditch the care
Pronto!!
And what people
Will I meet?
Family, neighbours,
Friends and foes.
Who knows yet,
At eight-oh-nine,
Where the Today Train goes?

God does!
Thank God!

With love from Karen

Part Eight

Christmas, Easter and Pentecost

Seeking

Snowflakes.
Robins.
Tinsel and trees.
Glitter,
Holly
And Reindeer.
Is The Baby in the manger?

Access,
Visa,
Mastercard,
Switch,
Cash
Or debt and strife.
Where's The Baby in the stable?

Crackers,
Plum pudding,
Mince pies
And wine;
Stuffing -
Ourselves and the turkey.
Are there Wise Men anywhere?

Leaden skies
And scurrying feet,
Rush
And hassle. Stress.
Is there really Christ in Christmas?

Find Him - while you can.

Open our eyes,
Let us see.
Open our minds,
Let us know.

Open our hearts,
Let us love.
Open our hands
And let us receive
The gift of
Christ in Christmas.

With love from Karen

The Gift

O best beloved friends,
Once upon a time -
(As all good stories start) -
On a crisp, clear
Palestinian night,
When the stars were ringing
With a music all their own,
A pregnant girl,
Young Mary,
Knew her time was near.
(No legend this, nor myth,
But history and fact.)

Because she knew her God
So well,
The strange events,
The journey and the crowded inn,
The smelly stable,
Animals and all,
Seemed quite alright.
When angels come
And tell you things
You *just know* that all is well,
And part of God's great plan for man.
So quite serene and calm
And radiant with joy,
Young Mary,
With Joseph there to help,
Gave birth
To her very special son.

And in that moment there began
The great desire of man,
To give at Christmastime.
The angels started first:
They gave the news
To startled shepherds on the hills.
Then the shepherds must needs give
Their worship to the lovely baby boy.
After them the kings,
Came with gifts
Of gold, and myrrh, and frankincense.

But in our haste to give,
Let us make time
To still our hearts
And take
God's precious *gift to us*.

With love from Karen

Light in the Dark

Christmas.
Lights in the darkness.
Angels and fairies,
Santa and stars.
Myths and legends,
And History.
His Story.

All was quiet and dark.
Outside
The moon
Shone her silver light
On frosted snow.
Total silence in the house.
The family slept,
All but me, that is.

The clock chimed six
As I crept downstairs.
My feet were bare,
The house stone cold,
But excitement warmed my toes.
The door was open
Just a crack,
And I crept in.

With sense of awe,
I saw the tree.
The Disney fairy lights were lit.
(It was fifty years ago!)
They twinkled
In the darkness of the room,
Casting a glow
On the fir green branches
Of the little tree

That we children had hung
With pretty baubles,
All those years ago.

Parcels lay below,
All neatly stacked
And labelled,
A gift for each.

So, I thought,
He's been.
Father Christmas came!

And, satisfied,
I climbed the stairs again
To wait
Till it was time.

O that we would all
Know that sense of awe.
O, that each would find
That gift,
Labelled with his name,
That everlasting glow,
Of Light
That came at Christmas.

We wish you
Each and every one,
The blessings of Christmas
And our love.

With love from Karen

Just for a minute

Just for a minute
Listen.
Hark.
Just for a minute,
Turn off the sound.
Switch off the telly,
Silence the toys.
Shut off the racket
Of science.
Get rid of the noise
Of logic.
And hark!
Stop shopping
Till you're dropping
And
Just for a minute,
Watch the night sky.
Hark and hear
The herald angels sing
From beyond the stars
News of light
In our darkness,
News of peace
In our strife.
News that brought shepherds
To their knees
In terror and awe,
And yet brought joy
For us all
If we would but hark
In the dark
Of our noise.

With love from Karen

The Cross and The Rose

The bard wrote
"My love is like a red, red rose",
And so a rose must be
The only way
I know to say
"My love I give to Thee."

At the cross's foot
I lay it now
In all humility,
And beg you to accept my gift
And all it means to me.

But, Lord, *You* know
It's not only my love
That I lay down now
At the cross of Calvary,
But all my hopes
And all my fears,
All my pains
And prayers and tears.
I look at this rose,
This red, red rose,
As it lies on the white of the cloth,
And I find I've laid down
Some other things too
Along with my gift to You.

There's my lazy habits,
And unkind thoughts,
And my arrogant words
And selfish ways;
There's the times I've gossiped,
And cheated the law .....
Lord, *You* saw when I copied that tape!

Are my motives always so squeaky clean?
Does my pride not blind my eyes?

Lord, the more I look at this red, red rose
And think I'm giving a gift,
I see that my "gift" is a poor, poor thing
Compared to Your gift to me.

So all I can do
Is hold out my hands
And gratefully take your gift,
And come and be bathed
In the red, red blood
That **You** have shed for **me**.

With love from Karen

Wind Blows
(Pentecost Poem)

Wind blows.
Wind roars.
Wind whispers.
Wind whistles
Through nooks and crannies,
Finding its way
To penetrate the snuggest home.

Wind ripples water.
Wind rustles leaves.
Wind moans and cries in pain.
Wind tosses trees and makes them dance.
Wind stirs up a storm and drives the mighty waves,
Makes breakers crash on storm-lashed shore.

Wind tears at leaves
And strips the trees till they are bare,
Exposing naked branch and twig for all to see.
Wind cleanses,
Sweeping away all that's dead and done
And letting new growth start.

Wind cold.
Wind chill.
Wind warm.
Wind hot.
Wind cool.
Gentle wind, the merest hint of breeze,
Sighing, stirring the sleeping branches of the birch
To make it rustle,
A pleasant sound.
The tinkle of wind chimes.
Delicate, harmonious,
Delights a summer's afternoon.

Wind turns windmills,
So man can mill his grain
And light his house at night.

Wind rushes,
Whirling and screaming,
Howling,
Angry, loud.
Tornado. Whirlwind, tossing dust,
Creating havoc in its path.
Fresh start needed after that!

Cooling wind,
Soothing the weary traveller in the scorching heat
Of desert sun.

Chilling wind,
Freezing the waters of the lake,
Lets man walk on water –
Like Jesus did.

How mighty is this power at work,
Yet quite unseen it goes,
And out of our control.
'The wind bloweth where it listeth',
So says the Word of God.

And like the wind,
This mighty, unseen power,
The Holy Spirit comes
And works His power in us.

With love from Karen.

Pentecost Fire.

We kept the folded grave clothes.
'twas all we had of Him.
The cross lay empty now,
As was the borrowed tomb.

Life seemed bleak.
The shattered dreams
And stench of death
Drained life
Of all its meaning.

We all went home.

Bewildered still,
And numb with shock and grief;
Our hopes had come to naught.

Forlorn, depressed,
We went about our tasks,
Pondering Jesus' words.
And wondering
What had it been about?

We did hear rumours after that,
That He'd been seen alive!
But that was quite absurd!
A nonsense!
Wishful thinking at its best!

After fifty days
We went
With other grieving souls
Up to Jerusalem.
It was the Feast of Weeks,
That time of year

When we offered up to God
The first-fruits of our harvest.

With heavy hearts
And feet of lead we went.
We thought
The journey up to town
Would help us to return
To life as it had been before,
Might help us to forget.

So there we were,
All gathered in the square.
The air was curiously still,
The atmosphere was charged,
There was the strangest sense
Of expectation.
As people felt it,
One by one they stopped
And stood
Quite silent for a minute.

And then it came!
A sudden rush of wind.
A glorious gale it was!!!
Through the streets it swept,
Swirling dust around our feet,
Tossing the treetops overhead,
Fresh and cooling,
Cleansing all before it.

Then came the flames!
Tiny golden tongues of fire,
Flickering and dancing
Joyously
Atop the head
Of each Believer there!

Our fear and dread were swept away,
Our heavy hearts were filled at once
With such a peace and joy
That none could quite describe!
New life, vitality,
Confidence and Holy boldness
Poured in to timid hearts and minds.
Power from On High!
We felt it then
And found ourselves
Addressing total strangers
With words we'd never used before!

I, myself a humble Galilean girl
Of little education,
Was speaking to a Greek
In his own tongue!
And on that day he too believed
And found new life in Jesus!

My sister told an Elamite
In his own tongue –
She spoke it fluent as a native!
Each stranger there
Was told the Gospel message plain
In his or her own tongue.
Then Peter stood and told the crowd
And thousands heard
And turned to follow Christ,
That man of sorrows
Whose crucifixion
They'd applauded
So short a time ago.

Miracles and wonders followed,
Healings, restoration,
Bitter family feuds forgiven,

Benjamin and Eli friends again
After years of hurt and pain.
(They'd forgotten how it started!)

Those tiny tongues of golden flame
Burned bright and hot all day,
Refining us
Like precious metal
Till we were pure and clean.

Life would never be the same again.

Praise God! With love from Karen

Part Nine

Holidays

The Island

1

Fair Thursday, damp, grey dawn, and the low clouds hang heavily over the drowsy, sleeping city. Soft rain drips persistently from gutters and trees. The early morning light gives the impression that it was never really dark anyway, that feeling that you get only in June and July.

The trees are rich with their full summer dark green. This is my favourite time of the day as I step out of the front door and stand for a minute just looking and listening. The world is all brand new again, ready for what another day will bring. There is the distant roar of the city, incessant but now muted, the accumulated sounds of all the trains and planes and cars and machines, and it sounds like the far-away roar of the mighty breakers on our beach three hundred miles away on the island. It's half past five in the morning, but it's broad daylight already. In the field down below us there are some horses, quietly grazing beneath the trees.

Look further, beyond the Vet College farm, and I see the whole city spread out across the Strath of Strathclyde, houses, trees, high-rise flats, church spires, parks, factories, chimneys, roads, and then beyond to the hills on the other side, clothed with fields and woods, dotted with houses and farms and villages, and in the far distance the higher hills, this morning almost obscured by rolling banks of grey cloud .

There are the occasional twitterings of birds, but the full dawn chorus of springtime is quieter now, presumably because the birds, like ourselves, are feeling the responsibility of parenthood weighing too heavily for much frivolity. Beside me, my lovely fuchsia splurges in an uncontrolled mass of dancing red flowers, and the untamed rambling pink rose pushes its sweet-smelling way through the fuchsia. As I go down the steps I stick my face into a rose and breathe in childhood memories of my Granny's garden.

Memories. What was it that my friend Steven said about living on in memories?

Meanwhile, down in Crow Road, life begins to stir. A few people hurry to work or emerge from the newsagent's with their papers. The crows caw raucously in the trees, and I wonder to myself if that is how Crow Road got its name. My other Granny's house was called Crowhill, and that sound too brings back memories. No one else is coming in to work today, just Ian and myself because it's a holiday weekend. This day actually turns out to be one of our busiest, and it transpires that I cope single-handed with admirable efficiency (!!), but right now all is peaceful, quiet and unhurried. Ian bustles about loading the van, and then departs. I get the coffee-pot going, and as the wonderful aroma of coffee fills the morning air I lean on my half-door and dream dreams for a little while. I watch "my" tree, heavy with greenery and already forming berries for Autumn. The persistent drizzling rain drips off every branch and leaf onto the neatly cut grass below, and I wonder if trees think thoughts about all the things that go on around them. If trees could talk!!

All of a sudden a new sound cuts into my thoughts. Seagulls. Several of the big white and grey birds circle the street, crying out with their harsh sea voices, and finding a rubbish bag of tempting scraps they swoop down to investigate. Squabbling and squawking at one another, they fight over the goodies and attract more of their kind, till the air is filled with nothing else but their cries.

Memories flood back. "I must go down to the sea today, to the lonely sea and the sky, and all I need is a tall ship and a star to steer her by"

... Memories ... Who said we weren't having a holiday this year? ... Listen to the cry of the gulls, and shut your eyes. Fair Sunday, damp, grey dawn, and the low clouds hang heavily over the drowsy, sleeping city. Soft rain drips persistently from gutters and trees, the early morning light gives the impression that it was never really dark anyway, that feeling that you get only in June and July. The front door opens and the family emerge one at a time, carrying bundles and boxes, welly-boots, buckets, bedding, books, toys, food, crockery, cutlery, pots and pans. Henry Ford's door is wide open and he joyfully welcomes the family aboard once more, bulging at the seams by the time the family have packed everything in. Merely to set foot inside him is to be in a different world. Holiday. Sand, sea, wind, rain, sun .... weather!

2

No other vehicle in the world makes that particular sound as Ian turns the key in the ignition, unless it might be another very ancient Ford Transit caravanette. There is a sort of ping-and-wheeze as Henry wonders whether or not to start, a bit of a judder as his stiff joints give in to the inevitability of moving off down Maxwell Avenue just one more time, and then we're off, with the two youngest members of the family crouching low under their duvets in case anyone from Westerton should see them in this embarrassing mode of transport. Mind you, who would be around at 5.30 a.m. to see us? The reason for the early start is the habitual fear that Henry might break down and cause us to miss the ferry, or we might get caught in the traffic on the Loch Lomond road if we didn't get past that bit before the rest of the world starts moving.

First stop, the petrol station. You can't get far without that. More hiding from spies!! Better top-up the supply of sucky-sweeties too, principally to keep Mummy awake because she was packing all night and didn't get to bed until half an hour before it was time to get back up again. Will she ever change?

Another wheeze and judder and we're moving again, off into the damp grey morning, heading towards the mist shrouded hillsides of Loch Lomond, the rain easing off now, but welly boot weather all the same.

There is the occasional hint of tension as Daddy wonders if Henry will make it this time, and what was that funny noise coming from under the bonnet? Gradually the holiday atmosphere takes hold, and as the mist recedes, so do our worries, and Mummy's eyelids grow heavier and heavier, and even the sharpest of soor-plooms is not enough to stop her nodding off. Not even the still grey-blue beauty of the loch, and the lush greenery of the wooded hillsides resounding with cuckoo calls are enough to keep her awake on this part of the journey.

The gentle application of Henry's brakes nudges me awake to the realisation that we're past Crianlarich, and we've made good enough time to stop for a quick brew up of the kettle. How on earth did we manage to come this far, I enquire, and stiffly emerge to go round to the back door and rummage amongst the mountain of carefully packed boxes and baggage to find the tea while Ian brews the kettle. The totally wonderful and inimitable smell of the gas cooker being lit confirms for us that we are on holiday again.

Somewhere along the way we must have left the mist and clouds behind, because, as my mother used to say, there is enough blue sky to make a sailor's shirt, and everybody knows that means it's about to be a glorious day! There is even steam coming off the road! We pack everything back into Henry and trundle off again on the Road To The Isles. Trundle is a word that suits Henry's progress admirably.

Tyndrum, The Black Mount, Glencoe, Balachullish. Our first sniff of the sea for a year. Blue mountains on the other side of Loch Linnhe, the sea sparkling and glinting in the sunshine, white painted crofts surrounded by gardens full of roses and hollyhocks, boats and sailing dinghies bobbing about at their moorings along the seashore, fields of hay, fields of grazing highland cattle, and tourists of all shapes, nationalities and of every kind of financial status, in cars and caravans, motorhomes and caravanettes varying from the sublime to the ridiculous, but none quite like our Henry, and of course there are bikes, tandems and motorbikes, and everywhere happy campers looking as if they had enjoyed unbroken sunshine for weeks rather than just emerged from drookit tents after a night of torrential rain!

Onward we trundle. Past the affluent suburbs of Fort William which looks positively continental in the glorious sunshine, then into the Great Glen, with Ben Nevis towering massively over us, looking docile just now and belying the potential disaster of a rapid weather change.

At the turn-off to Loch Arkaig and Achnacarry there is the memorial to the commandoes. *Lest we forget.* The Road To The Isles continues past moorland and ben, loch and glen, wooded hillsides, crofts, farms, the Well of The Seven Heads (the gory story is recounted on every journey) and on to the side of Loch Garry where it is definitely time to stop for a picnic. It takes a bit of doing, but eventually we find a stopping place with No Other People. Like some kind of giant ladybird spreading its wings, Henry's doors all open and his roof is raised to expose his unique ice-cream parlour horizontal stripes of red and white, which along with his cobalt blue and white paintwork make him quite unique!

Food never tastes quite as good as it does in Henry Ford, and there are certain foods which are only ever eaten in Henry Ford. As the sun blazes down we all peel off a layer or two of jumpers and jackets, and once we've eaten go for a leg-stretch down at the water's edge, chuck a few chuckie stones, pick some wild raspberries, admire the view, and then pack ourselves away and set off again.

Now we climb up, up, and over the wild and lonely stretch to Loch Loyne and Loch Cluanie. I always wonder what these glens looked like before the Hydro Board filled them up with water. They look so lonely and scarred, a tribute to man's inhumanity to nature. The words "God-forsaken and forlorn, desolate and bleak" spring to my mind, and I ask myself whether God does really forsake a place, or any person indeed?

The word forlorn must surely be related to the German "verloren", meaning lost. Can a place or people ever be lost, beyond the notice of God, or do we, in our guilt at what we've done to our world and each other in our desperate search for progress just think that we deserve to be God-forsaken? Man's inbuilt conscience is a powerful force, however much he may try to deny its presence.

If these lochs and glens look like this in July, what must they look like in January? I can actually just remember Glen Garry before they built the dam, when the old road ran past the beautiful River Garry, and although the man-made Loch Garry is lovely, somehow one hankers for the old days, when roads were roads, cars were cars, and the Hydro Board hadn't changed everything.

Enough of this philosophising. On with the journey, or we'll miss the ferry. That only happened once in 20-something years of making this journey, and it was because Henry broke down. We had to be towed ignominiously to Fort Augustus to be fixed, but it all had a happy ending anyway.

Even the bleakest of places looks beautiful today in the blue and gold weather. When we get out of Henry for another leg-stretch there is the pungent and all-pervading smell of bog-myrtle, and delicate, electric-blue dragonflies dart all over the place to the accompanying sounds of grasshoppers. Somewhere above us a lark soars high, higher, highest into the blue and gold, singing her pure, liquid song. Heaven.

3

The next part of the journey takes us through the breathtaking magnificence of the mountains and lochs of Kintail, the stuff of the Scots Pictorial Calendar, and hotching with tourists. It's not that we're not bowled over by the sheer beauty of it all, but we know it so well. We are reassured to see it, but we must hurry on. We are by now aching to see our beloved island, and it's not far now. Eilann Donan Castle .. Kyle .. a not too long wait for the ferry .. this is the bit where we remember the slower, older ferry and the l-o-n-g wait, and then on the other side we remember Ossie's ice-creams and the time that we managed to block the plumbing at the bed-and-breakfast in Kyleakin with somebody's disposable nappies! It used to be such a long and arduous journey that we had to stop off for a night either at Plockton or Kyleakin. Plockton had (presumably still has?) palm trees and seems almost unreal. In those far away days, when our first two children were the same size as our grandchildren are now, the roads were single track with passing places, and journeys were something to be undertaken with time in hand for delays. There was a time when I didn't think that my four-months-on-the-way baby could possibly survive the bumps and shoogles of this stretch of the road (She's nearly 29 now and has a tenacity and determination which were surely bred by that journey so long ago!)

Kyle of Lochalsh has earned its place in history by being one of the places where I stopped off to buy myself yet another amazing woolly tea-cosy style hat to put over my head to keep a) my ears warm and/or b) the midges/sandflies out. Uig has a similar place in the history books. I am usually very organised, with lists containing everything you could possibly need or think you might need and then some more besides, but inevitably something vital gets forgotten, like matches, knickers, toothpaste or fish-slice!

Skye. Island of many temperaments - sometimes windswept, wild and wet, sometimes still and misty with midges, sometimes damp and drizzly with midges, or sometimes, like today, gloriously sunny and hot without a midge in sight. And always the Cuillins. First we come to the Red Cuillins, curiously harsh looking with their steep sides covered in slippery looking red scree. I wouldn't like to try climbing them. (Well, to be honest, I'm not wildly enthusiastic about climbing *anything.*) To see the Red Cuillins at sunset is quite something - fiery with red and gold light and long, dark shadows: you expect to see dragons emerge and circle them. Then we reach the Black Cuillins, dramatic and dark, but somehow I could imagine myself climbing one of them more readily! (given that I might be in a mountain-climbing mood that day!!)

However, enough of this! Skye is not "our" island, and we have a ferry to catch. Our island lies far to the west, faintly visible on the horizon and still nearly two hours across the sea, give or take McBrayne-time. McBrayne-time is the amount of time by which your ferry may be running late according to weather and engine failure, not to mention Her Majesty's British Army and sundry other ingenious excuses. Of course, nowadays it should be referred to as Cal-mac time, but that doesn't have the same connotations at all!

We pass the place where we have camped overnight several times, remembering various adventures as we go by, and then, at last, there is Uig on the other side of the bay, snuggling in below the steep cliffs. Little white houses, the hotel, the church, the youth hostel, all scattered amidst hayfields and thick clumps of trees. There is the pier, but as yet no ferry boat, so we are in time! Probably lots of time!!

We join the queue of booked vehicles, check in, brew up another cup of tea (trying in vain not to cause our children too much embarrassment with our antics), and prepare ourselves for a wait. We fill the time with walking around the pier, visiting the new loos that they've built since our last visit, and watching the general activity that goes on at the end of an island pier. We also scrutinize all the people and wonder where they're all going, and who they all are - locals, sons and daughters returned for holiday visits, army types and holidaymakers like ourselves. They'd better not be thinking of going to Our Beach! What actually amazes us is the fact that our island holds all these people without us ever meeting any of them on our travels. They are probably thinking the same about us.

In the old days, when the ferry was less reliable, we sometimes had some very long walks while we waited. The ferry had a lift and a turntable, and only a few cars (and even fewer lorries, caravans or buses) were taken on at one time. Nowadays the turnaround time is much less, thanks to the drive-on-drive-off design of ferry, but perhaps some of the adventure has been lost.

In even further back days, when I was very young, each vehicle was hoisted on individually by a crane and ropes tied round the car. My Dad used to get so fidgety when they were loading on any of his precious cars!! Heaven help the McBrayne's ferryman who dared so much as leave a tiny scratch on a car of his! Memories too of times when it was really stormy and each car had to be firmly lashed to the deck with sturdy ropes. Presumably this part still happens, since modern technology hasn't been able to control the weather! Thank the Good Lord for that small mercy!

Standing on the pier watching expectantly we see the ferry coming round the point and into the bay. Not long now, so we go and get ourselves all sorted out with books and flasks of tea and games to play while we're on the crossing.

Eventually it's our turn to drive on, and we get Henry safely settled on the car deck, then climb the steep companionway steps up to the lounge and observation deck. Impatiently we watch as the last cars and people come on board and the sailors untie the ropes. The engines give a thrust that reverberates through the whole ship, the seagulls suddenly appear from nowhere and start crying to one another, and we're away! At last!! There is a steady thrumming and throbbing of the engines, and we stand at the rail watching as the ship cuts her way through the deep bluey-green of the waves.

There are jellyfish in the water, large brown and pink ones, smaller clear purple, pinky and blue ones, much prettier. Someone is feeding the seagulls with bread crusts and they come swooping down to snatch the crusts greedily from the hand that feeds them. Sometimes they cry out so harshly, and I wonder if they are laughing at us mortals, these big grey and white birds who swoop and soar and strut so freely and fearlessly. At other times they hover almost motionlessly above us, crying with that strange sea-mew that is lonely, soulful, aloof. And then again they bob about on the waves like corks, unsinkable. Perhaps it's nice being a seagull.

Looking far to the west we can see the mountains of Harris, blue and mysterious. Just south of them, low and barely visible on the horizon, floats the outline of Our Island, North Uist, on the edge of the world and bathed in the afternoon sunshine. Skye slips away behind us, as we plough steadily through the sparkling waves, every minute taking us closer to our heaven-on-earth. The gulls' cries and the gentle throbbing of the engines soothe us so that by the time we have crossed The Little Minch we are ready for the different pace of life that awaits. Though the sea is glassy calm, there is that point where east and west meet north and south and you can feel the ship give a gentle pitch and roll at the same time, just momentarily, and then before we know it we are sailing smoothly past the rocky shoreline of Lochmaddy Loch, with the scattered houses and crofts of Lochmaddy clearly visible, and standing protectively behind them the North Lee and the South Lee, dark and rocky, although only a few hundred feet high.

The whole ship shudders as the engines are put into reverse to control her arrival at the pier. Like a shark opening its jaws the front end of the ship opens up to let us all drive out onto dry land, and at last!! we're there! I know what the Jewish people feel like when they arrive at last in Israel, and I want to kiss the ground to show God my gratitude for being brought safely once more to this dearest of places. Already we can smell the peat-smoke blending with the smell of seaweed, and draw in deep breaths just to reassure ourselves that we are really here at last. Bliss!

4

It is by now well into the afternoon, but the golden weather is still with us as we drive past all the familiar sights of Lochmaddy, the row of council houses and the bank, the hotel and "Wehavit" shop (which sells everything the passing tourist might or might not want, and a few things which he didn't know existed but, now that he knows, he does want, at least, his wife and children do), then the petrol pump, the post office, the court house and assorted crofts and bungalows.

It's not very far till we come to water, since North Uist seems on first sight to be ninety percent water. We'll never forget the first night that we arrived on Our Island, when our impression was that we didn't know how it could be so waterlogged and not have sunk long since. The previous year we had stood on the top of Roneval, the highest point on South Harris, and had looked across the Sound of Harris to North Uist and had seen that it appeared to be more loch and lochan than land, and also we had sat on "our beach" on Harris and, from underneath a rain cloud, had observed that the sun seemed to shine more often on North Uist than it did on Harris. There was a reason for this, of course, and this is because Harris is mountainous and North Uist is much flatter. I won't bore you just now with the good scientific explanation to do with air rising and things like that! (This is another way of saying that I can't actually remember.)

Our first journey to North Uist was with two small children, aged three-and-a-half and eleven months, and we had with us in the car enough equipment to stock an entire branch of Mothercare. This was in the days before Henry Ford became our holiday home, and we would stay in crofts that took in holiday visitors. It was still sufficiently "the old days" that it was a long and arduous journey, and we would leave the previous day in case of delays, and then, having got to Uig, guess what? - naturally, being the old days too, McBrayne's was running at least two hours late. "The earth it is the Lord's, and all that it contains, except the piers and ferry boats, and they are all McBrayne's."

It was still daylight when we got onto the ferry, but it was a filthy night, of the sort one normally expects at the beginning of the Glasgow Fair, with the rain beating down against the ship's windows, a good-going gale, darkness setting in early, plenty of pitching and rolling and plenty of green-looking passengers clutching paper bags just in case! As we left the pier at Uig we were sailing straight into gloomy dark clouds and heavy seas, without a hint of land anywhere ahead - we could have been sailing to America, for all we knew, or off the edge of the world altogether! Around midnight the ferry did its shuddering and juddering bit and we saw some sign of flickering lights, and we deduced that we had reached Lochmaddy. When the voice on the tannoy system told us to go and get into our cars, we did as we were told, blindly following the sailors' instructions - they could have been telling us to drive straight into the sea as far as we could see! However, we did find ourselves on a road which, for all that it was pitch dark, seemed to wend its way over, round and between water, added to which it hadn't stopped pouring with rain all night.

We just drove on and on into this wateriness until eventually we saw a light and, hoping that it was a house, we stopped to ask where we were! Unbelievably, we had reached our destination, the croft which was to be our home for the next two weeks, and there was a warm welcome from our landlady, another Mrs. Macdonald, who had tea and scones ready for us, and then comfortable beds. We were full of apologies for our late arrival, but we needn't have worried so much, because life on the islands takes account of McBrayne time, and since she hadn't seen any cars passing she knew that the ferry was late. As for the weather, had we made a ghastly mistake in our assessment of how much the sun shines on North Uist? Not at all! Totally refreshed by a sound sleep, we awoke the next morning to a blue sky, bright sunshine, and a fresh sea breeze, with everything looking brand-new. So began our love-affair with this remote Hebridean island which the passing of quarter of a century and many visits have only served to intensify.

Meanwhile, back to the present. We have an important visit to make before we can go to Our Beach. We must check in with George and tell him that we are here, and to prepare himself for intermittent invasions of his and Rosemary's house whenever it rains too much or our laundry gets out of control. Everyone should have a cousin like George, and the best thing George ever did was to find a wife like Rosemary, which is another story too and can only be told with their permission!

So we drive the nine or ten miles across the island, recognising each loch and lochan, every familiar bend in the road, every passing place, every mile of sun-warmed moorland dotted with freshly cut stacks of peat. We pass the turn-off for Locheport, and then we reach Clachan, with its shop, a few houses, the Church standing on its own overlooking the bay, then round the corner to the right, and there it is! George's croft, low and snug against all weathers, right beside the sea, all neat and tidy, and up beside the road is the Smoke House, which could be described as "George's fish shop", but is in fact a fish smoking and processing business which is run with the precision and technology you would expect from an engineer.

We park Henry at the door and all pile in to the shop to greet

Henry Ford beside the patch of Sea Rocket

Henry Ford with Alison and Kirsteen
and Ian washing the dishes

George. Our arrival at this time of the year is almost as certain as swallows heralding the arrival of summer, so George and Rosemary are not surprised to see us even though we didn't actually let them know we were coming since we said goodbye last year. A few customers are served, then the door is closed, with the sign telling you to "ring the bell and haud on a minute till he gets his wellies on", after which we go down to the house for a quick cup of tea before heading off to our real destination. The family have a quick check of the premises to see that everything is as it should be. Is the pianola still there for wet-weather entertainment? Any changes are noted and approved, and, with a promise to come and see them soon, we're off again. It is totally accepted that the promised visit will coincide with certain weather conditions, and when that happens, assuming that no other friends or relatives have prior claim, we will be given a warm welcome. It is, after all, a but and ben with not a lot of room, and we do tend to do a bit of a takeover which George and Rosemary very graciously permit.

At last we're on the final stretch of our journey. After a few miles of coast road which takes us past crofts and fields with the sea always beside us, we go over the Committee Road which cuts across moorland and peat bogs to Sollas. Reaching the sea once more we come to the vast expanse of white sand and blue-green sea at Vallay Strand, with a picture postcard view of the distant mountains of Harris and in the foreground a much photographed thatched croft. On past familiar houses, crofts, the church, the Co-op and the post-office, down the hill a bit, and where Sollas finishes Grenitote begins.

There's the phone box (how many times have we used that phone box?), and there's the track that leads down past several more croft houses to the beach - Our Beach. We bump along the track, almost able to put Henry on automatic pilot, so familiar does this feel. Finally round the last bend, with the dog from the last croft yapping wildly at us (surely he ought to know us by now!!), and -- Yes! We've timed it just right, the tide on its way in is still low enough to let us cross the ford. Gently does it, just in case! Splashing slightly, and over we go! Henry revs up a bit, we're on the firm white sand at last, and away we trundle again, on and on and on, past the well-known landmarks, an entrance into the machair on our left, a rusty old car on the grass, a bit of an old bed, some car tyres, the usual assortment of debris festooned in seaweed, not so much somebody's old rubbish as an accepted art-form in the highlands and islands, a natural part of the landscape. Driftwood is a bit rare here, so camp-fires are not very easily assembled. To our right, it being low tide, mile upon mile of white sand, on a day like today soaking up the warmth of the sun, so that by the time the tide has come in and shallowly covered this huge expanse of beach, we will have our own tepid swimming pool.

5

How can I describe the perfume that meets us when we arrive on our chosen spot, that corner which we found all those years ago and would claim as our very own? The nearest description is the smell of honey, and as we joyfully tumble out of Henry, the warm familiar smell hits us. It comes from the bed of sea-rocket, which we understand can be found only in this part of the world. A lovely pale lilac coloured flower, it withstands gale-force winds and lashing rain, high tides and sandstorms, and still comes up smelling sweetly. One year we found that it had been all but obliterated by sand piled over it, but we discovered that the previously sparse bed on the other side of the sand-dunes was flourishing instead. We guess that it has been around for many more years than we have, and that it will somehow survive.

This year we discover that a huge chunk has been eroded from the Corran, that long arm of sand- dune covered in maram grass which forms the northern boundary of our place. We learn later that there were some pretty fierce gales last winter, and wonder how the topography of the whole peninsula that we are on will change as the years go by. We take comfort from the fact that there was continuous habitation on this peninsula for the last 2,000 years up till about 1920, and it was shortage of fresh water that eventually drove them from Udal up to Grenitote and Sollas. Now the continuous habitation consists of ourselves, and even more remote, about a mile further on, accessible most easily by landrover or tractor (or foot), "the dig" -- the archaeology professor and his students and family who have been coming to Udal for twenty-odd years. Apart from them, our neighbours are rabbits and birds and seals, and once we saw an otter too .

Once out of Henry, we have to take a quick reconnoitre to see that all is well with our place. The Corran (to the north) has to be investigated first -- a quick walk through the long maram grass and up the sand-dunes to stand on the top and look northwards, across more white beach and intensely turquoise sea to the Harris mountains. The sea on that side is our most frequented swimming place as the water is deeper but still warm and very safe for children. The view on a day like today could compare with Greek islands, we're sure, not that we ever visited a Greek island. It's hot, and some of the family can wait no longer to go for a swim. A quick dive back to Henry for towels and bathing things, and the first swim of the holiday takes place.

Meanwhile Henry has to be organised for living in. The unique stripey roof is raised, the various boxes are unloaded onto the sand and then packed into suitable places, so that by the time the swimmers have had their warm bath in the sea, the smell of dinner cooking wafts out to greet them on their return. Henry's outside is then draped with wet towels and bathing suits, and everyone piles back in to enjoy cuppa soups and macaroni hot-pot.

The sun is sinking in the west as we finish dinner, and we still have to investigate our western flank.

When we arrived we had manoeuvred Henry so that firstly he was level and secondly he would be above the normal high-tide level. I will never forget one very wild and stormy night when we were in Henry for the first time. It was our first night on the beach, and although we had come for many years for picnics, the stormy night closing in on us was a new experience. We weren't sure how high the tide would come, nor were we sure whether Neil's little tent would withstand the gale-force winds, so Ian went over the dunes to share Neil's tent where it was pitched on the nearest grass.

Henry was fairly rocking back and forth with each gust of wind, and the girls and I felt quite vulnerable without our menfolk. As I peered out through Henry's curtains I could see the sea coming nearer, and nearer, and nearer. There was, of course, absolutely no danger, because as I have said, the bay is very shallow, so I resolved to stop being so silly, shut the curtain, and went back to what I was reading. At that time I was working my way systematically through some Bible reading notes with a passage for each day, and I was amazed at what I read next. Call it coincidence if you want, and call me naive, gullible and over-trusting if you want, but God spoke to me quite clearly that night: "... he (The Lord) gave the sea its boundary so that the waters would not overstep his command ... " (Proverbs 8.)

Now this is the same God who said to me when I became a Christian, "You shall know the Truth, and the Truth shall set you free." I was being set free from a small and irrational fear, and the next morning showed that the tide had indeed stopped just six feet short of Henry's wheels.

Many years later, staying in the same place, I was to know in a much bigger and more impressive way complete release from the captivity of the terrible fear of operations. On that occasion I was facing major surgery immediately after I returned from holiday, and all I felt was this fantastic peace about it all. It was "the peace that passeth all understanding", which I am not given to experiencing under normal circumstances, as my family will testify. I have a faith that, generally speaking, solves more problems than it creates.

(A passing thought: of the two aspects of faith, which is the more difficult - trust or obedience?)

On that first occasion with the tide it was as if God was asking me to trust Him in something small so that I could learn to trust Him in something bigger when my faith had grown stronger. On our journey home from that pre-operation holiday God gave us an added bonus: at around midnight, after a very delayed journey we stopped to camp overnight near Ardelve and saw the most incredible display of the Aurora Borealis that you could ever hope to see. The wonder of that night stayed with me for many days, and the "peace that passeth understanding" stayed with me all the way through my visit to hospital. I didn't need even as much as a sleeping tablet the night before the operation!

However, we are supposed to be investigating our western flank, so we walk into the unbelievable colours of the setting sun, up the deeply rutted track through the bank of sand dunes till we reach the top and look the half mile or so across the machair-covered peninsula to the high ridge of dunes that overlooks the three-mile stretch of Traigh Iar, "the west beach."

Traigh Iar is The Most Wonderful Beach In The World, but a little impractical for Henry-living, so we compromise by living on Traigh Ear, "the east beach", which is more sheltered and more accessible, but still near enough to hear the mighty waves breaking on Traigh Iar, incessant and timeless as God Himself. We can walk over every day just to drink in the beautiful view, or to have a more exhilarating swim. As we walk over the machair the millions of bunny-rabbits bob their white tails in warning to each other as they take off, bounding and leaping towards their multitudinous warrens so fast that they nearly fly!

Walking over the machair is like walking on a carpet of flowers. Wherever the crofters have left a neat rectangle of cultivated land to lie fallow it seems that a different colour of flower has chosen to grow, so that you have one patch of forget-me-nots, another of white daisies mixed with red poppies, yet another with bright yellow flowers, and another with yet a different mixture of colours, harebells, vetch, wild orchids and buttercups. All the time there are birds of all kinds, curlews, skuas, oyster catchers, sea-gulls, and the dear little ones that we call "clockwork boidies". Sooner or later I will be inspired to chant my second holiday poem. The whole recitation has to be said in one breath: *"the common cormorant or shag lays eggs inside a paper bag the reason you will see no doubt is to keep the lightning out but what these unobservant birds have failed to notice is that herds of wandering bears come with buns and steal the bags to keep the crumbs."* This, along with the MacBrayne jingle, forms my entire repertoire of memorised verse as I have a useless memory for such things. I can remember lots of telephone numbers, car registrations and the like, but not words.

It is the end of a long and satisfying day, so we go back to Henry, and when we put on the light inside it now seems much darker than we had thought when we were outside in the last remnants of evening light. The gas is lit under the kettle, we brew up the last cup of tea for the day, and out come the traditional chocolate biscuits, which we would never dream of having at home. A discussion ensues as to which packet we should open (all part of the traditional evening tea ceremony in Henry.) Is it to be Gold Bars or Penguins, Classics or Jacob's Club? Certain members of the family have refined to perfection the art of slicing chocolate covered biscuits with a knife to make them last longer than anyone else's!

Living in Henry Ford is simple, but only so long as a simple routine of tidiness is followed, so we tidy away all the dishes and the bedtime routine gets under way. First the bunks are unfurled and slotted into place and the occupants settled with sleeping bags and assorted baggage. At this point the atmosphere becomes a little fraught with tension. (We are a highly-strung lot, and tiredness brings out the worst in some of us.)

Tooth brushing takes place outside by the light of the moon, and having done that I stand there waiting while poor Ian, as usual, gets left with the chore of assembling our bed (an ingenious arrangement of the table and bench seats). Then he comes out too, and we just stand together looking at our domain. The lights of the village and the township twinkle cosily, snuggled into the side of the hill and over there the slightly incongruous glow of streetlights marks the biggest group of cottages.

Over to the east the moon casts her cool white light over the odd shape of Crogary Mor and makes a path over the waters which now almost completely cover the sand of Traigh Ear. Crogary Mor is the highest point at this end of North Uist, and is all of 180 metres high! If we turn around and look westwards we can still just see the night blue of the sky fade to a faint green against the uneven horizon of the huge sand dunes that run the three mile length of Traigh Iar. Somewhere over there in the isolated solitude of a couple of wooden huts, beside some very ancient remains at the "dig", the professor of archaeology may or may not be in residence, and beyond that the setting sun is on its way to America. And always there is the sound of the sea on Traigh Iar.

We climb back into Henry, and very tired and very happy, we snuggle down under the duvet and drop into a deep, contented sleep.

Sometime in the middle of the night I hear our cat at the window and am already halfway out of bed to go and let her in when I realise that it is the mewing cry of a lone gull in the dawn, and I drop off to sleep again, enjoying all over again the contentment of being here once more.

6

We are awakened quite suddenly by the unmistakable sound of the landrover coming over the track through the dunes. The professor must be in residence. I peek through the curtains, and sure enough, the landrover emerges and heads off up the beach towards Grenitote. He is not limited as we are by the times of the tides, and we have in the past watched enviously as he charged through the deep water while we waited for the tide to go down far enough. In the early days we nearly missed dinner on more than one occasion because we weren't wise enough! Now we watch smugly as other strangers are caught, but we are not unkind enough to let them wait without the offer of a cup of tea and a chat. We have also gone to the rescue several times when strangers got stuck in the soft sand beyond our place, (that's why we don't go any further!!), and have met some very interesting people that way.

I have a good stretch and then lazily snuggle down again to snooze and just enjoy the sensations: first and foremost there is the persistent, consistent and insistent buzz of two or three sandflies that have managed to sneak in the small opening in the window. Sandflies! I could write a book about the delights of sandflies and our totally useless, but sometimes quite ingenious, methods of trying to get rid of them. I wonder if they laugh at us as much as we are irritated by them. Bless their little wings, they get everywhere you can think of, and a few places you didn't think of too! -- and they tickle! Their buzzing can drive you to dementia, if you let it, but eventually we have learned to live with it, at least most of the time. This is one of the reasons that not many people frequent our beach. If they only knew it, however, there are no midges here. Perhaps the sandflies have eaten all the midges. Or perhaps they drove them insane. Maybe insane midges bite more than sane ones. Perhaps if I had never gone to North Uist I might be a normal person, not given to bouts of scattiness and lunacy. Ah well, it's too late now!

The sun is beating down out of a cloudless blue sky, and already it is beginning to get quite hot inside Henry. There is a curious pattering sound on the roof. It can't be rain, so what is it? I lie there listening and trying to establish the cause of the sound, and then I notice that there is something moving on the opaque red skylight above my head. It is the cutest thing! – it's the upside down view of the bottom of the tiny feet and claws of a "clockwork boidy", of which there must now be quite a flock pattering around over our heads! One of the children stirs and makes a movement, so I quickly look out of the curtains again just in time to see the little birds take off. Strangely enough, while they are so comic to watch on the ground, once they are airborne they are completely graceful.

Time to get up!! This is a reverse action of the bedtime routine and takes a little while. It's not so bad if we can all get out while the routine is performed, but if it's pouring with rain and blowing a gale then it can be distinctly fraught with tension. Today it's easy, and before long we are all dressed and in our right minds, sitting down to a long leisurely breakfast with many cups of tea, not to mention, for me anyway, a good book to read. Ian is more energetically inclined and wants to go for a walk -- all the way to the nearest sheltered spot on the other side of the dunes, where he will lie and sun himself in the company of the sandflies. The family find various ploys, and I sit and read with yet another cup of tea for a while until the buzzing sandflies drive me out. Before I go, I tidy away the dishes - even housework in Henry's compact living space is enjoyable. Why can't I keep my house like I keep the inside of Henry, I ask myself.

We have a very limited supply of water - strictly rationed for tea and coffee and tooth brushing, and occasionally for cooking. Whenever possible we even cook with sea-water -- porridge and potatoes get cooked in 50-50 sea and fresh water. One feast which we will always remember consisted of smoked trout accompanied by new potatoes boiled in sea-water. The trout and potatoes were all from George's. I guarantee that no restaurant on earth could have pleased us better.

Dishwashing, you will now understand, is something else again. We load the dishes (of which we use as few as we can) into a bucket and simply wait for high tide! As the water has by then become quite warm, it's quite a pleasurable occupation, splashing around in the waves with the plates floating away from you in all directions! If it's wild and stormy I wear my wellies and woolly hat for this operation, and then it's hard work catching the plates and mugs as they not only float away on the tide but also get blown away down the beach, and have to be rewashed because they are all covered in sand! A fortnight of this mode of dishwashing is the only cure I know for dry and sensitive skin, and I always return home with hands like a princess!

We while away the morning, happily occupied with these activities. Round about lunchtime (peanut butter and plum jam) Ian observes that a front is coming in, and sure enough there is a layer of barely discernable thin white cloud, very high, just beginning to threaten our sunshine. After lunch it is noticeably cooler, and the wind, which very rarely stops blowing anyway, has veered round and chased away the sandflies. It is time to go for a walk, and we decide to go and see if we can find again the ancient spring of fresh water round on the headland a mile away, along Traigh Ear and near the old ruined church and cemetery. Armed with the water-can we set off, over the dunes and onto the second stretch of Traigh Ear.

Just here is the place where, when the children were very small, we used to picnic regularly. We can still picture the four of them, Alison leading the way, marching round and round with their arms outstretched, chanting "mill, mill, mill, mill" and laughing uproariously. We can't really remember what it was all about, but the image is imprinted on our minds forever!

Here is the place where you must walk with your eyes glued to the sand because several times we have found cowrie-shells here. Once you start looking for treasures like these, it's amazing how many interesting things you find. The sand is so fine and white, and there are dozens of the pretty little shells that are like pink butterflies' wings.

The tide is quite low now, and the sky is grey. All of a sudden the wind carries a sound to our ears that is now familiar, but which at first we used to find a little disconcerting. It is the haunting, mournful call of the seals. It is so like a human cry that it is little wonder that legends abound in Celtic folklore of the silkies, the creatures that are part human, part seal, and whose descendants have their first and second toes webbed. Sometimes as we walk along this beach we are accompanied, at a safe distance, by one or two seals, but not today. They have even been known to come and watch us as we swim.

On another occasion we walked out over the sands at low tide to the rocks where the seals live, and found a whole colony of them watching us with their huge, gentle eyes, until we got a little too near them, at which point they slipped gracefully into the water and disappeared.

We find our little spring, marked unobtrusively by a cross carved into the rocks at the base of which the water appears, miraculously fresh just above high tide level, and clean enough for us to fill our can. If we collect water this way, it saves us making the journey back to civilization at Sollas, where the co-op has an outside tap for us to fill Henry's tank.

Later on, after dinner, we set off again for the high dunes above Traigh Lar. The wind has died down a bit, and the sandflies abound in the long jagged marram grass. We reach the place that we regard as our own lookout place, and while the children wander off down to the beach to paddle and hunt for treasure, Ian and I just sit together and watch.

Perched up in a sheltered hollow, about thirty or forty feet above the beach, like a pair of eagles in an eyrie, we survey the world. This was the place where little Alison and little Neil played while little Catriona lay asleep in her yellow carrycot, ensconced between two clumps of grass where she wouldn't slither all the way down to the bottom of the dune. Then a couple of years later, little Catriona joined her big sister and brother playing on the beach below and little Kirsteen slept in the carrycot up here beside, us. And now they are all grown-up, and grandchildren will no doubt come and play on the beach next year with us, please God. As we sit together in our eyrie, we marvel at all the wonderful things that have happened in the last thirty years, and we thank God, and trust Him for the next thirty.

With love from Karen,
for Ian on the occasion of our
30th Wedding Anniversary,
28th September 1993

Endword

Well, there you have it. My thoughts and feelings on life in general, traumas and trivialities, as seen through the eyes of a daughter, grand-daughter, big sister, wife, mother, cousin, niece, aunt, grandmother, and I hope friend of many. I have been surrounded by love all of my life and would seek to share that with others who haven't been so blessed.

My parents and grandparents had strong Christian faith, so it was not unnatural that I should follow that road, and as a small child I remember being introduced to Jesus as 'an elder brother'. I liked that idea as I really wanted a big brother! (My mother did do her best to oblige by producing four little brothers and a little sister!) It wasn't until I was 35 years old, however, that I suddenly understood that I couldn't inherit faith from the previous generation, but had to appropriate it for myself. I saw this transaction with God as me getting out of a car, handing over the ignition key to Jesus, and me getting into the passenger seat and letting Him take control over where the car was going, and when and how! The resulting journey has led to what you have read in this collection.

Now you must be wondering what on earth Mothmilk and Moondust means as a title. Let's discuss 'moondust' first. I asked my husband what he thought the name implied, and the response was 'fairytale', 'sparkling', 'airy-fairy'. I think that pretty well covers it! My mind is full of moondust, pretty sparkling stuff, not quite down to earth at all, and inclined to be scatter-brained and absent-minded! When my mind is up there, that's when the poetry gets in!

As for mothmilk, well, that goes back to the inescapable fact, as witnessed in my Sugar-Dragon poems and 'Another Day, Another Diet', that for 54 years I have been 'on a diet'. Being a prodigious tea-jenny, I've always consumed a lot of milk in my many large mugs of tea. Therefore, to reduce the calorie intake that this habit involves, I usually have in the fridge a jug made up of half skimmed milk and half water. Sounds revolting, doesn't it! For many years this concoction was kept in a bottle in the door of the fridge, and it had a label on it reading 'Mother's Milk'! If you half-turn the bottle in the door, all you can see of the label is 'Moth Milk' … hence the family name 'mothmilk' for my concoction. So, now you can understand, my obsession with weight control is a large part of my psyche (if you'll forgive the pun!)

I thank God for my sense of the ridiculous, and I hope that my title encapsulates the peculiar dichotomy between tragedy and comedy that makes life so enchantingly full of humour amid pathos, and which enables us to journey onwards through the difficulties, knowing that there is hope around the corner.

Postscript

by *John Miller*, *former Moderator of the General Assembly
of the Church of Scotland*

Karen Macdonald's enchanting book casts its own spell. It contains the most delicate of thoughts woven together with historic events which have the force of earthquakes. The book is a tribute to family life, to parenthood and childhood, a celebration of life and faith. It contains both an account of lyrical joys, and a lament for a life extinguished young. In Karen Macdonald's poems and essays honest questions about evil and death stand beside tributes to the generosity and kindness of one person to another. Who could fail to be moved by the tragic tale of doomed love, the idyllic marriage of Olwen and the wartime death of her young husband, Spitfire pilot Duncan McCuaig; by the drama of the story of his last flight emerging fifty years after his death, or by the tribute to the role played by a stepfather in the life of his adopted daughter?

Now in a further tribute to her mother Olwen Drysdale, Karen Macdonald has devoted any proceeds from the sale of this book to the work of the Strathcarron Hospice. Olwen received advice and care from the Hospice, as an in-patient and an out-patient, over a period of ten years until her death in 1994.

Admiring what Karen Macdonald has written I am honoured to write these lines in praise of her book, and having myself seen the Hospice caring for a dear friend I am glad to commend Karen's hope of raising funds for its work.

Strathcarron Hospice

Strathcarron Hospice opened in 1981. The hospice movement was in its infancy in the 1970s but a local doctor, Dr Harold Lyons, having observed the sufferings of many patients in their last days, was convinced that 'there must be a better way of dying.' He formed a group of people with similar understanding, and when a suitable private house, Randolph Hill, came on the market, they bought it and started the Hospice. In the years since then Strathcarron Hospice has established itself as an integral part of medical care in the Forth Valley.

At any one time some four hundred patients are under the care of the Hospice. The Hospice provides what is known as 'palliative' care. When a medical condition is such that no further improvement is possible, the Hospice offers all-round caring for the patient and their family. There is a Ward with 24 beds, and patients may stay just overnight, or for indefinite longer periods.. Each week sees one hundred patients coming for day-care. There is a team of six Nursing Sisters who visit patients in their homes. The Hospice has an Education Department where four Nurse Tutors teach the principles of palliative care to District Nurses, care workers from homes and hospitals, and students from Glasgow and Stirling Universities.

Most of the patients of the Hospice are from the Forth Valley. But if their relatives live within easy visiting reach of the Hospice, patients may come from any part of the country to be cared for in Strathcarron.

A Place of Life

Many people associate the very word 'Hospice' with thoughts of death. On the contrary however, as Mr Bob Blewitt of the Hospice staff says, 'Hospices are all about living, living to the best of your ability for as long as you can.' For this reason the Hospice has craft courses and occupational therapists. A Social Worker is on the staff to help patients and families to draw on the social resources of their local communities. A full-time Chaplain is in post, to assist people in reflecting on the spiritual issues which arise at the prospect of death. And families who have accompanied their relatives through their last days are always welcome to return to the Hospice in the future for discussions and advice.

Karen Macdonald and her family have remained grateful to the Hospice and its staff for all they did for Olwen. They hope, now, that this book may in some measure continue to express their and Olwen's gratitude.

Strathcarron Hospice,
Randolph Hill
Denny
Stirlingshire
FK6 5HJ

Karen McCuaig Macdonald.

Born in September 1942, right in the middle of the war, like so many other Scots destined by circumstances to be born 'abroad'. Because my father was doing wartime photographic reconnaissance from R.A.F. Benson near Oxford, I made my first appearance in Didcot, Berkshire.

Because of the war, I lived at twelve different addresses in the first eighteen months of my life, finally settling at age 4 in Killearn, Stirlingshire, where my parents came from. Then Glasgow, Dunblane and finally Dollar. I went to several different primary schools, but was very happy to settle down to my senior schooling at Dollar Academy. After a brief and confused year at St. Andrew's University I came to Glasgow where I got married to Ian (who had been born in Yokohama, Japan), and we have lived in the same house in Bearsden, Glasgow ever since, for 41 years now. We have four children and six grandchildren, and our totally chaotic home is 'home from home' to them and my brothers and sister, nieces, nephews, cousins and friends.

Ian and I are both active elders in the church we go to in Drumchapel, and my hobbies are reading, listening to music, writing, photography, computer graphics, travel, tatting, 'Kumihimo' (Japanese braiding), beadwork and goodness knows what next!! I also try to fight the flab by going to the gym ... reluctant to go, but enjoy it once I'm there.

Printed in the United Kingdom
by Lightning Source UK Ltd.
102538UKS00001B/251